Ban Billionaires

Also from EATMS Productions

Books on power, survival, women's autonomy, and the systems shaping modern America.

Nonfiction

Billionaires, Capitalism, and Power

Evil and the Mountain Ungreed
Self Help for American Billionaires
Selfish Steve and the Ivory Tower
Tariffs, Taxes, & Face-Eating Leopards
Ban Billionaires: Fascism Fix

Fascism, Religion, and Cultural Control

Self Help for the Manosphere
Fascism 2025
Fascism & the Perverts & the Greed Virus
Christian Fascism Marriage Book
Tyranny, Table Manners, & Tiramisu

Guides for Women's Autonomy and Protection

How to Survive in Post-America as a Woman
Project 2025 American Drag
4B – Burn, Ban, Boycott, Build
4B OG – So No Go GYN
I'm Glad He's Dead

Analysis of Authoritarian Project 2025

Project 2025: The Blueprint
Project 2025: The List
Project 2025, Christian Dumb Dumbs, & The Republican Agenda
Fascism, Project 2025, & The Pinkprint

Modern Rewrites for Women

Stoic Principles Reimagined
Siddhartha Reimagined
The Prince Reimagined for Women
The Art of War Reimagined for Women
The Jungle Reimagined
The Constitution Reimagined for Women

Machine Learning Series

AI, Bitcoin, Nostr for Women
AI, Safety, & Security for Women
AI, Anxiety, & Health for Women
AI, Kids, & Family Safety for Women
AI, Creativity, & Personal Expression for Women
AI, Independent Work, & Parallel Power for Women

Social Systems Series

Emotional Labor for Women
Household Power for Women
Workplace Power for Women
Medical Bias for Women
Aging Systems for Women
Recovery Systems for Women

Fiction

Dystopian Stories of Resistance and Collapse

Propaganda Paige & the Missing Prosperity
Propaganda Paige & the TIDE Manifesto
Propaganda Paige & the Shadow Cartographers
Propaganda Paige & the Prosperity Alliance
Propaganda Paige & the Shattered Truth
Propaganda Paige & the Rising TIDE
Propaganda Paige & the Last Bastion
Propaganda Paige & the Dawn of Prosperity
Project 2025: Dorian — The Last Men
Project 2025: Boy — A Last Men Novel

Ban
Billionaires
Fascism Fix

Appropriate Response 1

by
Esme Mees
& Mary Schiele

EATMS
PRODUCTIONS

ISBN 978-1-966014-10-2

Cover, interior design, interior prints by: Esme Mees

eatms@pm.me
www.eatms.me

Check out EATMS Underground:
https://tinyurl.com/eatmsNOSTR

Printed in the United States of America.

Socialism never took root in America because the poor see themselves not as an exploited proletariat but as temporarily embarrassed millionaires.

— John Steinbeck

$1 vs. 1 Billion

A single $1 bill is approximately 0.0043 inches thick. Here's how they stack up:

A Million Dollars in $1 Bills

Stack Height: A million dollars in $1 bills would be 358 feet tall.

Comparison: That's about the height of a 30- to 35-story building or just taller than the Statue of Liberty (305 feet from base to torch).

A Billion Dollars in $1 Bills

Stack Height: A billion dollars in $1 bills would be 67.9 miles (358,000 feet) tall.

Comparison:
That's 11 times the height of Mount Everest (29,032 feet).
It extends well into the upper stratosphere, nearing the mesosphere, where meteors begin to burn up.
For context, the stratosphere starts at around 6 miles and ends at 31 miles, so a billion-dollar stack reaches more than twice as high as the stratosphere's upper limit.

Side-by-Side Metaphor
A million-dollar stack is like standing next to a tall skyscraper, impressive but comprehensible.
A billion-dollar stack, on the other hand, soars into space, dwarfing Mount Everest and entering layers of Earth's atmosphere that most people only dream of reaching.

This striking difference highlights how mind-bogglingly large the jump is between a million and a billion dollars!

Table of Contents

Introduction
Class Warfare
Us vs. Them

The billionaire class, the apex predators of capitalism, are not merely wealthy individuals, they are the crowning achievement of a system designed to hoard wealth, power, and influence for the few at the expense of the many. Their very existence is a testament to the moral and societal rot that festers beneath the veneer of modern democracy. They are not innovators; they are hoarders, gatekeepers, and parasites, whose empires are built on the backs of those they exploit. Their wealth is not a sign of success but a glaring indictment of a system that rewards greed over humanity, extraction over creation, and destruction over sustainability. We must not be fooled into believing that these individuals represent the pinnacle of human achievement. They are not aspirational figures, they are warnings, evidence of what happens when a society loses its moral compass and surrenders to the seductive lies of unbridled capitalism.

While billions struggle to meet their basic needs, the billionaire class thrives in grotesque excess. They live in mansions the size of small towns, sail superyachts that dwarf naval vessels, and hoard wealth that could eradicate poverty many times over. Meanwhile, their factories pollute the air, their investments raze forests, and their policies keep wages stagnant and conditions dire for the workers who make their fortunes possible. The stark juxtaposition between their lifestyles and the reality faced by the majority is not just an economic disparity; it is a moral chasm. They tell us that their wealth is a reward for their ingenuity and hard work, but we know better. Their wealth is built on the deliberate suppression of ours. This is not left versus right; it is us versus them, the many versus the few who would see the planet and its people consumed for their own insatiable appetites.

The complicity of political institutions in this systemic robbery cannot be overstated. Republicans, unabashed in their servitude to corporate interests, have built their platforms around ensuring the unfettered accumulation of wealth for the already wealthy. Tax cuts for the rich, deregulation of industries, and the relentless assault on unions and workers' rights, these are their hallmarks. Yet, the Democrats are no better. They are the wolves in sheep's clothing, offering performative opposition while quietly capitulating to the same masters. They speak the language of reform but legislate in service of the same donors who bankroll their campaigns. The landmark 2010 Supreme Court case Citizens United was not an anomaly; it was the culmination of decades of bipartisan complicity in the erosion of democracy and the consolidation of power by the billionaire class. When both sides of the aisle are bought and sold, who is left to represent us?

This betrayal runs deep. Policies that gut public trust, from austerity measures to the privatization of essential services, are not accidents; they are deliberate. These politicians have built a machine that ensures the survival of the wealthiest at the cost of everyone else. They have starved public schools while funding tax breaks for corporations, allowed healthcare to become a profit-driven nightmare, and turned housing into a speculative asset rather than a basic human right. And they have done all this while cloaking themselves in the rhetoric of democracy, freedom, and progress. But there is no progress here. There is only the deepening of inequality, the hollowing out of our institutions, and the slow, suffocating realization that the system is not broken, it is working exactly as it was designed. For them.

We find ourselves adrift in a society that has abandoned leadership in favor of servitude to wealth. This vacuum of moral and ethical guidance has left the populace disoriented and cynical, deliberately stripped of the tools needed for collective action. Despair is not a natural state; it is cultivated by those in power as a means of control. Cynicism is their weapon, wielded to ensure that we never believe in the possibility of change. "This is just the way it is," they say, as the cost of living rises, wages stagnate, and the planet burns. "Nothing can be done," they whisper, while lining their pockets with the fruits of our labor and the spoils of our land. They rely on our resignation. They count on our hopelessness. But we know better. We know that this is not a natural order; it is a carefully constructed lie. And once we recognize it as such, we can begin to dismantle it.

The psychological toll of living in a society dominated by billionaire wealth is immense. We are bombarded daily with stories of rising costs, stagnant wages, and environmental collapse. These are not just economic issues; they are existential threats that weigh heavily on our collective psyche. The constant barrage of bad news creates a sense of hopelessness, a feeling that no matter how hard we work, we will never get ahead. This despair is not accidental; it is deliberately fostered by those in power. A population that feels powerless is less likely to organize, to demand change, to fight back. And so, we are left adrift, abandoned by leaders who have failed to address the systemic rot at the heart of our economy. But this is not the end of the story. Throughout history, transformative change has come from unexpected places, ordinary people rising up to challenge oppressive systems. The question is not whether leadership will emerge from this chaos, but whether we will recognize our own power to create it.

The billionaire class thrives on our despair. They rely on our belief that the system is too big, too powerful, too entrenched to change. They want us to believe that opposition is futile, that the best we can do is survive. But this is a lie. The power of the billionaire class is not absolute; it is fragile, dependent on our compliance. If we withdraw that compliance, if we organize and demand change, we can dismantle the structures that sustain their wealth. This is not a call for violence or destruction; it is a call for collective action. It is a call to build a movement that challenges the status quo and demands a better world.

The first step in this process is to reject the narratives that have been imposed on us. We must reject the myth of the self-made billionaire, the idea that wealth is a sign of virtue and poverty a sign of failure. We must reject the notion that the system is fair, that anyone can succeed if they just work hard enough. These narratives are tools of control, designed to keep us in line. They are lies, and they must be exposed as such. Only then can we begin to imagine a different world, one where wealth is not concentrated in the hands of a few but shared by all.

The path forward is not through reliance on corrupted institutions but through grassroots opposition. History is filled with examples of ordinary people coming together to challenge systems of oppression. The labor movements of the early 20th century, the civil rights struggles of the 1960s, the environmental activism of today, all of these were driven by people who refused to accept the status quo. They did not wait for leaders to emerge; they became the leaders. They organized, they protested, they demanded change. And they succeeded, not because the system was willing to accommodate them, but because they forced it to. The same is true today. The billionaire class may seem untouchable, but their power depends on our compliance. If we withdraw that compliance, if we organize and demand change, we can dismantle the structures that sustain their wealth.

The tools for this revolution are already at our disposal. Social media, for all its flaws, has given us the ability to connect and organize on a scale that was previously unimaginable. Grassroots movements like Occupy Wall Street and the Fight for $15 have shown us the power of collective action. And the growing awareness of the climate crisis has created a sense of urgency that transcends borders and ideologies. These are the building blocks of a new movement, one that challenges the billionaire class and demands a more just and equitable world.

But this movement will not succeed without sacrifice. It will require us to step outside of our comfort zones, to confront the systems of power that have shaped our lives. It will require us to take risks, to face backlash, to endure setbacks. But the alternative is unthinkable. If we do not act, the billionaire class will continue to exploit us, to hoard resources, to destroy the planet. The stakes could not be higher. This is not just a fight for economic justice; it is a fight for the survival of our species.

Lastly, we must recognize that what billionaires are doing is not just immoral, it is fascism in its most refined, corporate-controlled form. The wealthiest individuals on the planet do not need to march in uniforms or deliver fiery speeches to command absolute power. Instead, they buy influence, rewrite laws, and reshape economies in their favor, all under the guise of legality. They manipulate governments, fund think tanks to manufacture consent, and bribe politicians who eagerly do their bidding, ensuring that the laws designed to curb their excesses are either dismantled or never written in the first place. This is how fascists have always operated, not by openly declaring themselves as tyrants, but by embedding themselves within the structures of power until they become indistinguishable from the state itself. Billionaires do not need to seize power by force because they have already purchased it.

The trajectory we are on is not just one of economic inequality or environmental collapse, it is a full-speed descent into a new kind of fascism, one where corporate empires dictate the terms of governance, where public institutions serve private interests, and where the very idea of democracy is rendered meaningless. This book will explore precisely how this consolidation of wealth and power follows the classic fascist model: the fusion of corporate and state interests, the destruction of labor rights, the use of mass surveillance to maintain control, and the violent suppression of any who dare to resist. History has shown us where this path leads, but the difference now is that we are seeing it unfold at an accelerated, technological pace, with billionaires wielding power more absolute than many dictators of the past. This *is* class warfare: us vs. them, greed vs. goodness.

The morning light filtered weakly through the soot-streaked windows of the factory, casting long shadows over the rows of humming machines. Each grinding, clattering piece of equipment seemed to echo the same relentless monotony as the lives of the workers who tended them. Among them was the man whose hands moved with a practiced efficiency that belied the weight of exhaustion etched into his body. He had worked in this factory since he was seventeen, starting as a boy full of hope and vigor, but now, at forty-six, his back was stooped, and his face bore the deep grooves of a lifetime spent in servitude to the rhythm of machines that were never his own.

The factory was his entire world, not by choice but by necessity. Each day was a carbon copy of the one before: the deafening roar of machinery, the acrid smell of oil and molten metal, the unforgiving glare of fluorescent lights that turned even the brightest day outside into a sterile shadow. It was here that he earned the pittance that kept his family clothed and fed, here that his sweat and labor built the wealth of a billionaire he had never met and likely never would. The man worked tirelessly, knowing that the fruits of his labor would never be his to enjoy, that every widget he produced added another drop to an ocean of wealth he could never access. He represented the backbone of a system that thrived on his toil while offering him nothing but crumbs in return.

Home was not far, though it felt a world away. The man's partner, a woman worn by years of hard work and harder disappointments, stood in the small kitchen of their modest house. She moved methodically, preparing dinner with a precision that came not from joy but from necessity. Every meal was a calculation, every decision about what to buy and how to stretch it another small battle against the relentless tide of bills and rising costs. She once believed in the promises of politicians and corporate managers who assured her that hard work would pay off, that their sacrifices would lead to a better life for their children. But those promises had long since soured, leaving her with only the bitter taste of disillusionment.

Their child sat at the kitchen table, their wide eyes fixed on a battered schoolbook. The child was young, curious, and quietly observant in a way that often unsettled the adults around them. They asked questions that went unanswered or were brushed aside with a vague "That's just how it is." But the child could not accept that. They wondered why their father came home so tired, why their mother's hands were always rough and red, why their home was so small while the factory owner's mansion loomed at the top of the hill, visible from nearly every street in town. These questions nagged at them, planting seeds of curiosity and, unknowingly, opposition.

The family's home was modest and tidy, its walls lined with photographs that told a story of endurance rather than prosperity. In one, the man was a young boy standing beside his own father, a man who had worked in the same factory decades before. The boy in the photo had dreams of escaping the factory, perhaps becoming a teacher or an artist, but the pull of necessity had been stronger than the pull of dreams. When his father grew too old and frail to work, it fell to him to step into the factory's grinding maw and keep the family afloat. The same pattern had played out across generations, a cycle of exploitation passed down like an unwanted heirloom.

The man remembered his father's stories vividly. He remembered sitting at the kitchen table, much like his own child did now, listening to tales of the strikes and protests that once shook the town. His father had spoken with a mix of pride and bitterness about the times when the workers had risen up, demanding fair wages and decent conditions. For a while, they had won small victories, a few cents more per hour, an extra day off each month, but those gains had eroded over time, chipped away by managers and politicians who knew how to divide and conquer. By the time the man had started working at the factory, the unions were a shadow of their former selves, their leaders co-opted or silenced.

Now, sitting at the same kitchen table where he once listened to his father's stories, the man felt the weight of history pressing down on him. He saw it in the weary eyes of his partner, in the quiet questions of his child, and in the factory that loomed in the

distance, its smokestacks belching gray plumes into the sky. The cycle of exploitation was unbroken, the promises of a better future unfulfilled. And yet, as he watched his child's furrowed brow and intent expression, he felt the faintest flicker of hope, a fragile ember that maybe, just maybe, the cycle could be broken.
The child's questions were not confined to the walls of their home. At school, they noticed things that others seemed to ignore. The textbooks spoke glowingly of industrial progress and economic growth but said little about the lives of the workers who made that progress possible. The child noticed that their classmates who came from wealthier families, the children of managers and business owners, seemed to move through life with an ease and confidence that felt foreign to them. They began to see the invisible lines that divided their world: the lines between wealth and poverty, between power and powerlessness, between those who built and those who profited.

One evening, as the family ate dinner, the child asked a question that hung heavy in the air: "Why does the factory owner live in such a big house while we live here?" The man and his partner exchanged a glance, a silent conversation passing between them. "That's just how it is," the man said finally, his voice heavy with resignation. But the child was not satisfied. They pressed on, their questions becoming sharper, more insistent. Why was it "just how it is"? Who decided it had to be this way?

The partner tried to steer the conversation elsewhere, sensing the tension that was building, but the child's words lingered. Later that night, as the man sat alone at the kitchen table, he thought about those questions and felt a pang of guilt. He had once asked the same things, had once dared to dream of a different life. But those dreams had been ground down by the weight of reality, leaving him with only the grim determination to keep going, to survive.

As the child lay awake in their small bedroom, they thought about the mansion on the hill and the factory in the valley. They thought about their father's tired hands and their mother's weary eyes. They thought about the lines dividing their world and wondered what it would take to erase them. The answers did not come that night, but the questions would not go away. They would grow, taking root in the child's mind and heart, shaping their view of the world and their place in it.

The narrative shifts back to the factory, its smokestacks silhouetted against the setting sun. The machines hum and clatter, oblivious to the lives they consume. The man's hands move with the same practiced efficiency, but his mind is elsewhere. He thinks about his child, about their questions, about the faint flicker of hope he had felt. He wonders if it is foolish to hope, if the cycle can ever be broken. But he also wonders what might happen if the next generation refuses to accept "that's just how it is." Perhaps they will find a way to do what he and his father could not. Perhaps they will find a way to rise.

Breaking the Illusion: The Factory and the Robber Barons of 2025

The factory stands as a stark microcosm of capitalist exploitation, a grim emblem of a system that thrives by extracting wealth and labor from the many to enrich the few. The hum of machinery, the sweat of workers, the relentless grind, these are not just features of an industrial space; they are the foundation upon which billionaires have constructed their empires. This is not an abstraction. It is not a relic of history. This is the machinery of 2025, still churning, still consuming lives, and still lining the pockets of the few who orchestrate it from a distance, untouched by the ruin they create.

The factory's purpose has never been to uplift the workers who keep it alive. It exists to generate profit for its owners, who remain invisible to those whose labor fuels their obscene wealth. Workers' bodies are worn down, their families stretched to breaking, while the billionaire class sits on unimaginable fortunes, shielded from accountability by layers of legal protections, lobbying, and carefully crafted illusions of benevolence. The factory's smokestacks, billowing with pollutants that choke the air and poison the land, are not just scars on the environment, they are symbols of a broader betrayal, one that sacrifices both human dignity and the planet's future for short-term profit.

This betrayal is systemic, deliberate, and pervasive. It is a machine designed to funnel wealth upward, where it collects in vast, stagnant pools, never flowing back to the workers who created it. The billionaire class has mastered this design, ensuring that the system remains rigged in their favor. They have perfected the art of profiting without accountability, reaping rewards while outsourcing risk, avoiding taxes, and shifting blame. They do not build; they hoard. They do not innovate; they extract. They are not visionaries; they are parasites, leeching vitality from every corner of the world they touch.

This is not progress; it is robbery. The billionaires of today are no different from the robber barons of history, except that they've traded the railroads and oil fields for tech empires and private equity portfolios. They have rebranded themselves as innovators, disrupters, and philanthropists, hiding their greed behind a carefully curated facade of progress and public good. The media they control glorifies their so-called genius, turning them into icons of aspiration while erasing the suffering they cause. Their self-serving narratives dominate the cultural landscape, framing their accumulation of wealth as inevitable, even virtuous, while casting the workers who sustain them as expendable.

Consider the language they use: they are "job creators," as if the labor of their employees is a gift bestowed upon them rather than a transaction designed to maximize their own profit. They are "innovators," as if the exploitation of workers and the destruction of ecosystems are necessary sacrifices for the greater good. They are "philanthropists," as if the crumbs they drop from their banquet tables can replace the systemic change needed to address the inequities they perpetuate. These narratives are not just lies; they are weapons, wielded to maintain their dominance and to keep the rest of us docile and compliant.

But these myths are crumbling. The facade of benevolence is cracking under the weight of its own contradictions. In a world where billionaires hoard unimaginable wealth while homelessness and hunger persist, where private jets pollute the skies while communities drown in rising seas, where the cost of living skyrockets while wages stagnate, the truth becomes impossible to ignore. Their wealth is not a mark of brilliance but a scar on society, a grotesque testament to a system that prioritizes greed over humanity.

Opposition begins with seeing through the illusions. It begins with rejecting the narratives that glorify billionaires and accepting the reality that their wealth comes at a devastating cost. It begins with recognizing that they are not the solution but the problem. And history tells us that opposition is not only possible; it is inevitable. The labor movements of the past, the civil rights struggles, the fight for environmental justice, all of these were born from moments of profound inequality and injustice, just like the one we face now.

These movements were not led by the powerful or the wealthy. They were led by ordinary people who dared to imagine a different world, who refused to accept the status quo, who saw the cracks in the system and used them as leverage to bring it down. Leadership emerges not from the halls of power but from the streets, the communities, the factories. It emerges from those who are closest to the pain, who understand the stakes because they live them every day.

We are living in a moment ripe for such leadership. The billionaire class has overplayed its hand, pushing the system to a breaking point. The contradictions of their wealth and power have become too glaring to ignore. Their narratives of inevitability and invincibility are unraveling, and the collective anger of those they exploit is rising. The question is not whether opposition will come but when and how.

This opposition will not look like the movements of the past. It will be shaped by the tools and technologies of our time, by the interconnectedness of a world where ideas can spread in an instant and where communities can organize across borders. It will be fueled by the creativity and resilience of those who refuse to give in to despair, who see the cracks in the system not as barriers but as opportunities.

The fight ahead is not just about survival; it is about transformation. It is about building a world where wealth is not hoarded but shared, where power is not concentrated but decentralized, where progress is not measured by profit margins but by the well-being of people and the planet. This is not a utopian dream; it is a necessity. It is a matter of survival for humanity and the Earth itself.

And so we must dare to imagine. We must dare to believe that the system can be dismantled and rebuilt, that the factory can be transformed from a site of exploitation to a space of creation and empowerment, that the billionaires can be toppled from their pedestals and replaced by a world that values humanity over greed.

This is the call to action.

This is the beginning of a movement. This is the moment where we recognize our power and rise to meet the challenge. The TIDE is rising. The time is now.

Esme Mees & Rita Shelby, Winter 2025

TIDE: Target, Inspire, Disrupt, Empower*

Target identifies the core systems, institutions, and individuals responsible for perpetuating inequality and harm. Whether it's corporations funding destructive policies, lawmakers blocking progress, or systems exploiting marginalized communities, targeting shines a spotlight on these forces, holding them accountable. It ensures that the fight for justice is focused, strategic, and unrelenting.

Inspire reminds us that no movement can thrive without hope and connection. Storytelling, art, and collective action ignite passion and solidarity, transforming despair into determination. Inspiration is the fuel for progress, reminding us why we fight and what we can achieve together.

Disrupt recognizes that oppressive systems rely on compliance. By disrupting their rhythms, through boycotts, strikes, protests, and civil disobedience, we expose their fragility. Disruption is not chaos; it is a calculated refusal to accept the status quo, a strategic challenge to entrenched power.

Empower is the culmination of TIDE, focusing on creating systems that uplift and sustain communities. Empowerment ensures that as we dismantle unjust structures, we build resilient alternatives: participatory democracy, mutual aid networks, and inclusive governance. It is the process of returning power to the people, ensuring that progress is not temporary but permanent.

TIDE is a clear and aggressive plan to tear down systems built on greed and oppression. Politicians have proven, time after time, that they cannot be trusted. They choose greed and self-interest over the people they are supposed to represent. TIDE demands we target the roots of injustice, inspire people to act together, disrupt the power structures that keep us oppressed, and empower communities to take control of their own futures. The ultimate goal is to eliminate the need for politicians altogether, replacing them with technology that allows us to govern ourselves, fairly, transparently, and directly. Liberation is not a dream; it is the path we are building.

Reclaim Direct Democracy: Defund Congress*

TIDE (AKA *The Pinkprint*) envisions a future where governance belongs to the people, free from the inefficiencies and corruptions of the current congressional system. Congress, as it operates today, often stands as a barrier to progress, a structure entrenched in outdated norms and dominated by corporate lobbying and partisan power plays. Rather than serving as a tool for democracy, it has become a bottleneck, where the interests of the few override the needs of the many. In this vision, we oppose this stagnation by redefining governance itself, using technology to create a decentralized, transparent, and participatory democracy that bypasses traditional gatekeepers.

The foundation of this transformation lies in dismantling the financial and institutional grip that allows Congress to operate as a machine for special interests rather than public good. By defunding the excessive mechanisms that perpetuate congressional power, such as exorbitant campaign financing, lobbyist influence, and outsized administrative costs, we shift resources back to the people. This doesn't mean dismantling governance altogether; it means reallocating its purpose. Funds previously tied to maintaining the status quo can be redirected toward technological infrastructure that enables direct citizen engagement in decision-making. Imagine a system where policy is not dictated by a handful of lawmakers but actively shaped by millions of voices in real time.

This evolution hinges on technology. Secure platforms, built on blockchain and other decentralized systems, can facilitate direct voting, policy proposals, and public discourse, ensuring that every citizen has a tangible role in governance. These platforms would eliminate concerns of fraud or manipulation, using encrypted verification systems to authenticate identities while protecting privacy. Every citizen, regardless of socioeconomic status, would have equal access to shaping the laws that govern their lives. In this model, Congress no longer serves as the sole legislative body; it becomes obsolete, replaced by a participatory democracy that is as dynamic and adaptable as the people it serves.

Critics may argue that direct democracy at this scale is impractical, citing concerns over misinformation, low engagement, or logistical challenges. *TIDE* (AKA *The Pinkprint*) acknowledges these obstacles but frames them as opportunities for innovation, not excuses for inaction. A robust framework for civic education will accompany this technological shift, ensuring that citizens are equipped with the knowledge to engage meaningfully. Transparent algorithms and independent oversight can guard against misinformation campaigns, while gamification and incentives encourage participation. The goal is not just a functional system but an engaged citizenry empowered to shape its collective destiny.

This vision is not a call for chaos but a demand for accountability. Traditional representative systems often centralize power in ways that make it difficult for citizens to hold leaders accountable. Direct democracy disperses power, returning it to the hands of the people. With no intermediaries, there is no room for the influence of corporate lobbyists or backroom deals. Policies are debated openly, decisions are made collectively, and power flows from the ground up. The act of opposing corruption becomes built into the system itself.

At its heart, this shift represents more than a technical upgrade to governance, it is a philosophical revolution. It challenges the assumption that a small group of elected officials can adequately represent the will of an entire population. Instead, it affirms that the collective wisdom of engaged citizens, equipped with the right tools and education, can govern more effectively and equitably. This is not a rejection of democracy but its evolution, where representation is replaced with participation, and leadership becomes about facilitation rather than control.

The *TIDE* (AKA *The Pinkprint*) vision of direct democracy is not only achievable but necessary in the face of entrenched inequality and systemic failures. By opposing the inefficiencies and inequities of the current system, we open the door to a government that reflects the true will of the people. Defunding Congress as it stands today is not about dismantling democracy, it is about liberating it, transforming governance from a distant institution into a living, participatory process. Together, through innovation and collective action, we will build a system where power is not hoarded but shared, where decisions are not dictated but debated, and where democracy is not a privilege but a right. Ending fascism starts with ending greed.

*Pages 25-28, As Outlined in *Fascism, Project 2025, The Pinkprint*, Esme Mees & Luna Max, From the Series *Our Future* 1, 2025.

Create a list of ideals and values to fight for below:

Chapter 1
The Myth of Meritocracy

The myth of the self-made billionaire is one of the most pervasive and dangerous lies of our time. It is a narrative meticulously crafted to obscure the structural advantages, inherited privileges, and systemic exploitation that underlie immense wealth. We are told these individuals are geniuses, pioneers, and icons of innovation who pulled themselves up by their bootstraps through sheer grit and determination. But this is a fairy tale, one that props up the billionaire class while keeping the rest of us in awe of their supposed achievements. The reality is far less glamorous. Billionaires are not born from ingenuity alone; they are born from systems rigged in their favor. They inherit not just money but networks, connections, and access to opportunities that most people can only dream of. They benefit from tax loopholes, subsidies, and policies designed to protect and expand their wealth. Their success is not a testament to the free market or the American Dream; it is an indictment of a system built to concentrate wealth and power in the hands of the few at the expense of the many.

Consider the historical and contemporary figures often held up as paragons of self-made success. Andrew Carnegie, the 19th-century steel magnate, is frequently lauded as the epitome of the American Dream. Yet his rise was fueled by ruthless exploitation of workers, including those who labored under grueling and dangerous conditions in his steel mills. His wealth was built on the backs of people whose lives were cut short by the demands of his empire. Fast forward to the 21st century, and we find Elon Musk, a man celebrated as a visionary entrepreneur. But Musk's rise was not a solitary journey of brilliance; it was paved with millions in family wealth, government subsidies, and exploitative labor practices. These are not isolated examples; they are the rule rather than the exception. The so-called self-made billionaires are, in reality, the beneficiaries of systemic advantages and the architects of systems that perpetuate inequality.

The media plays a central role in perpetuating this myth. Stories of billionaire triumphs dominate headlines and documentaries, turning individuals into cultural icons while erasing the systemic forces that made their wealth possible. We are inundated with rags-to-riches tales that conveniently omit the threads of privilege and exploitation woven through these narratives. The media's glorification of billionaires serves a dual purpose: it legitimizes their wealth and power while shifting the blame for systemic failures onto individuals. When we are told that anyone can succeed if they work hard enough, the logical conclusion is that those who struggle must not be trying hard enough. This bootstrap ideology is not just a lie; it is a weapon, wielded to divide us and to keep us from questioning the system itself.

The bootstrap myth is especially insidious because it is so deeply ingrained in our culture. It tells us that success is a matter of personal effort, that the only barriers to wealth and prosperity are laziness and lack of ambition. But what happens when we examine this myth through the lens of reality? We see a landscape littered with systemic barriers: wage stagnation, unaffordable healthcare, crumbling infrastructure, and an education system that prioritizes profit over learning. These are not individual failings; they are structural realities, designed to keep wealth concentrated at the top while leaving the rest of us to fight over scraps. The bootstrap myth shifts the burden of failure onto individuals, absolving the system of any responsibility and keeping us focused on personal shortcomings rather than collective solutions.

The media's complicity in this narrative goes beyond glorification; it actively obscures the harm caused by the billionaire class. For every story about a billionaire's charitable donation, there are countless untold stories about the lives and communities devastated by their wealth accumulation. When Jeff Bezos donates a fraction of his fortune to a charitable cause, the media praises his generosity while ignoring the warehouse workers collapsing from exhaustion or the small businesses crushed by Amazon's monopolistic practices. When Bill Gates funds a new initiative, the headlines celebrate his philanthropy while overlooking the systemic issues that his business empire exacerbated. These stories are not just omissions; they are deliberate distortions, designed to protect the reputations of the wealthy while keeping the rest of us in the dark.

The harm caused by this narrative is not limited to economic inequality; it extends to our collective psyche. The constant glorification of billionaires creates a culture of aspiration that teaches us to admire wealth rather than question its origins. It normalizes exploitation, framing it as the price of progress, and it fosters a sense of individual inadequacy in those who struggle to make ends meet. This psychological toll is profound. It keeps us divided, demoralized, and distracted, ensuring that we remain too preoccupied with our own perceived failures to see the system for what it truly is.

The myth of the self-made billionaire is not just a lie; it is a barrier to progress. As long as we believe in it, we are complicit in our own exploitation. We are taught to see billionaires as the pinnacle of human achievement rather than as symptoms of a system that prioritizes greed over humanity. This myth keeps us locked in a cycle of admiration and envy, preventing us from imagining a different world. But we can break free from this cycle. We can reject the narratives that glorify wealth and instead embrace the values of equity, solidarity, and justice. We can challenge the structures that sustain inequality and demand a system that works for all of us, not just the few.

To dismantle this myth, we must start by questioning the stories we are told about success and failure. We must recognize that wealth is not a measure of virtue and that poverty is not a sign of moral failing. We must understand that the barriers we face are not of our own making but are the result of deliberate choices by those in power. And we must reject the idea that our worth is tied to our productivity or our ability to accumulate wealth. Our value as human beings is inherent, and our society should reflect that truth.

The fight against the myth of meritocracy is not just about exposing lies; it is about reclaiming our power. It is about understanding that the billionaire class thrives on our compliance and that we have the ability to withdraw that compliance. It is about building a movement that challenges the status quo and demands a better world. This is not a fight we can afford to lose. The stakes are too high, and the consequences of inaction are too dire. We must dismantle the myths that divide us and instead build a narrative of solidarity, one that unites us in the pursuit of justice and equity.

The billionaire class is not invincible. Their power is not absolute. It is built on a foundation of systemic inequality, and that foundation can be dismantled. But it will not happen on its own. It will require us to question the narratives we have been fed, to organize and demand change, and to imagine a world beyond the constraints of greed and exploitation. The path forward is not easy, but it is necessary. The myth of the self-made billionaire has held us captive for too long. It is time to break free.

The myth of meritocracy thrives not only on the glorification of billionaires but also on the deliberate policies that entrench their power. These policies are not accidents or oversights; they are carefully crafted mechanisms designed to ensure the continued concentration of wealth and the suppression of opportunities for everyone else. Tax cuts for the wealthy, deregulation of industries, and subsidies for corporations are not just economic strategies, they are acts of class warfare, waged against the majority to protect the interests of the few. These policies create a feedback loop where wealth begets more wealth, and power becomes more deeply entrenched. They erode public trust, hollow out social safety nets, and leave communities struggling to survive under the weight of systemic neglect.

Consider the tax structures that allow billionaires to pay a smaller percentage of their income in taxes than the average worker. These loopholes are not anomalies; they are features of a system designed to privilege wealth over work. Offshore accounts, carried interest exemptions, and capital gains tax rates are tools that billionaires use to shield their fortunes from public responsibility. Meanwhile, the burden of funding public services falls disproportionately on those who can least afford it. This is not just an economic injustice; it is a moral failure, a betrayal of the social contract that should bind us together.

Deregulation is another cornerstone of this system. Under the guise of promoting innovation and growth, deregulation strips away protections for workers, consumers, and the environment. It allows corporations to cut corners, exploit labor, and pollute with impunity. It prioritizes profit over people, turning communities into collateral damage in the relentless pursuit of wealth. The billionaire class champions deregulation because it removes the few remaining barriers to their accumulation of power. It is a tool of domination, a way to tilt the playing field even further in their favor.

Subsidies for corporations are often presented as investments in economic growth, but they are, in reality, handouts to the wealthy. These subsidies funnel public money into private hands, enriching billionaires while leaving essential services underfunded. The rationale for these subsidies is always the same: they will create jobs, stimulate the economy, or promote innovation. But the promised benefits rarely materialize. Instead, these subsidies deepen inequality, diverting resources away from schools, healthcare, and infrastructure to pad the pockets of the already wealthy. This is not just bad policy; it is theft, a redistribution of wealth from the many to the few.

The cumulative effect of these policies is the erosion of public trust. When people see billionaires thriving while their own communities are left to decay, they lose faith in the institutions that are supposed to serve them. This erosion of trust is not a side effect; it is a deliberate outcome. The billionaire class benefits from a disillusioned and disengaged populace. When people lose faith in government, they are less likely to demand change. They are more likely to accept the status quo, to believe that nothing can be done. This cynicism is a weapon, wielded to suppress dissent and maintain the illusion of inevitability.

But the illusion is fragile. The cracks in the system are becoming impossible to ignore. The cost of living continues to rise, wages remain stagnant, and the climate crisis looms ever larger. These realities expose the lie at the heart of the myth of meritocracy. They reveal a system that is not fair, not just, and not sustainable. The billionaire class may seem invincible, but their power is built on a foundation of lies. And once those lies are exposed, their power begins to crumble.

The path forward requires us to rethink our assumptions about success and wealth. It requires us to reject the narratives that glorify billionaires and to embrace a vision of economic justice that prioritizes people over profit. This is not a call for incremental reform; it is a call for systemic change. It is a call to dismantle the policies that enable inequality and to replace them with policies that promote equity, solidarity, and sustainability.

We must demand a tax system that holds billionaires accountable, that ensures they pay their fair share and contribute to the public good. We must fight for regulations that protect workers, consumers, and the environment, that prioritize safety and well-being over corporate profit. We must challenge the subsidies that enrich the few at the expense of the many, redirecting those resources to the communities that need them most. These are not radical ideas; they are necessary steps toward a more just and equitable society.

But policy alone is not enough. The fight against the myth of meritocracy is also a cultural battle, a struggle to change the way we think about wealth and success. We must reject the idea that billionaires are role models, that their accumulation of wealth is something to aspire to. We must celebrate the contributions of workers, educators, caregivers, and activists, the people who truly make our society function. We must redefine success not as the amassing of wealth but as the creation of a world where everyone can thrive.

This is not an easy task, but it is a necessary one. The billionaire class will not give up their power willingly. They will fight to protect the system that benefits them, using every tool at their disposal to maintain their dominance. But history shows us that change is possible. The labor movements of the past, the civil rights struggles, the fight for environmental justice, all of these were battles against entrenched power, and all of them achieved victories that once seemed impossible. These movements remind us that the power of the many can overcome the power of the few.

36

The first step is to recognize our own power. The billionaire class may seem untouchable, but their power depends on our compliance. If we refuse to play by their rules, if we organize and demand change, we can dismantle the structures that sustain their wealth. This is not just a fight for economic justice; it is a fight for the humanity of our society. It is a fight for a future where wealth is not concentrated in the hands of a few but shared by all, where opportunity is not determined by birth but by potential, where the economy serves the people rather than the other way around.

The time for action is now. The cracks in the system are growing, and the myth of meritocracy is unraveling. We have the tools, the knowledge, and the collective power to build a better world. But it will not happen on its own. It will require us to challenge the narratives that divide us, to organize and demand change, and to imagine a world beyond the constraints of greed and exploitation. This is our moment. This is our fight. And it is a fight we can win.

The Weight of a Day

The factory roared to life each morning with a sound that was both familiar and oppressive, a deafening reminder of the hours to come. The worker moved through the cacophony with a practiced rhythm, their body attuned to the demands of machines that never rested. Each step, each motion, was calculated for efficiency, not comfort, as though the factory itself demanded tribute in the form of sweat and fatigue. The air was thick with the smell of oil and metal, a scent that clung to skin and clothes long after the day's work was done. The floors vibrated faintly beneath their feet, a constant hum that seeped into their bones.

This was the worker's world, one they had known since their youth, though familiarity had not bred acceptance. The factory was a place where time stretched and collapsed, each hour dragging on but disappearing into the void of repetition. The worker's hands moved almost instinctively, guiding raw materials through the machines, shaping them into the components that would be shipped off to places they would never see. These parts would become someone else's profits, someone else's innovation, someone else's empire. For the worker, there was no sense of pride or ownership in what they created, only a grim acknowledgment that this labor was what kept the bills paid and food on the table.

The factory floor was a study in monotony. Row upon row of identical workstations, each occupied by a figure hunched over their task, created a sense of isolation despite the crowd. The worker often glanced around, catching brief glimpses of their colleagues. There was Sam, whose limp grew more pronounced with every shift but who couldn't afford to take a day off. There was Clara, a mother of three who often looked as though she hadn't slept in weeks. There was Ahmed, a recent immigrant who worked harder than anyone but rarely spoke, his face a mask of quiet determination. They were all bound by the same invisible chains, each one a cog in the massive, unyielding machine of capitalism.

The worker's thoughts often wandered during the long hours, even as their hands remained busy. Today, they thought of their child, who was likely just arriving at school. They imagined them sitting at a desk, their small hands clutching a pencil, their face alight with curiosity. The worker's heart ached with a mixture of pride and sorrow. They wanted more for their child than this, more than the factory, more than the endless grind of labor that offered so little in return. They wanted their child to dream big, to believe in possibilities that felt so distant in this town dominated by the shadow of the factory.

But dreams felt like a luxury the worker couldn't afford. Their own aspirations had been ground down over the years, eroded by the constant demands of survival. They remembered a time when they had imagined a different life, one where they could create something meaningful, where their work would be valued not just for its output but for its impact. Those dreams had faded, replaced by the grim pragmatism of making ends meet. The worker couldn't help but wonder if their child's dreams would suffer the same fate. Would they grow up to feel the same weight of entrapment, the same sense of being a small, replaceable piece in a system that cared nothing for them?

The factory itself felt alive in its indifference. Its walls bore the marks of decades of wear, its machinery clattered and groaned with age, and its lights flickered occasionally, as though mocking the people who toiled beneath them. It was a place that consumed and discarded, offering no gratitude for the lives it sustained. The worker thought of the owner of the factory, a man whose name they barely knew but whose wealth and power loomed over every aspect of their life. That man, comfortable in his mansion miles away, untouched by the noise and grime of the factory floor, would never know their name. He would never feel the ache in their shoulders or the exhaustion that settled deep in their bones. He would never understand the sacrifices made to build his fortune.

The lunch break offered a brief reprieve, though even this felt like part of the grind. The worker sat at a metal table in the break room, their meal a hastily assembled sandwich and a bruised apple. Around them, conversations ebbed and flowed, voices low and cautious. They talked about rent increases, medical bills, the rising cost of groceries. Occasionally, someone would mention a news story about the owner's latest venture or acquisition, their tone a mix of bitterness and resignation. The worker listened but said little, their thoughts still with their child.

As the afternoon wore on, fatigue set in. Each motion became heavier, each breath a little harder. The clock seemed to mock them, its hands creeping forward at an agonizing pace. The worker's mind drifted to their partner, who was likely at home managing the household, a job that was no less demanding than the factory. They thought of their family as a team, each doing their part to keep things afloat, though the weight of the system bore down on them all. The worker often wondered how long they could keep this up. They thought of Sam's limp, Clara's exhaustion, Ahmed's quiet determination. They thought of the countless others who had passed through this factory over the years, their lives shaped and often broken by the demands of the job.

As the shift finally ended, the worker felt a fleeting sense of relief. They walked home through streets lined with houses much like their own, their body aching but their mind focused on what awaited them. When they arrived, their child greeted them with a smile, their small arms wrapping around them in a hug that seemed to momentarily lift the weight of the day. The worker looked into their child's eyes and felt a glimmer of hope, fragile but persistent. They knew the challenges that lay ahead, the barriers that seemed insurmountable. But in that moment, they allowed themselves to believe, just for a second, that their child might find a way to escape the cycle, to build a life beyond the shadow of the factory.

As the family sat down to dinner, the worker listened to their child talk about their day, their questions and observations filling the room with a kind of light that the factory could never provide. The worker's partner joined in, their voice warm but tinged with the same quiet exhaustion that marked all their days. Together, they shared a meal and a moment of connection, a brief respite from the demands of the world outside. But even as they laughed and talked, the worker couldn't shake the thought that lingered at the edge of their mind. They looked at their child and wondered: Would this cycle ever truly end? Could they break free, or were they destined to walk the same path, their dreams ground down by the same relentless machine?

The worker's gaze lingered on their child, who had grown quiet, their focus now on a drawing they had started at the kitchen table. The worker recognized the factory in the sketch, its smokestacks rising against the sky, but there was something different. The smokestacks were surrounded by trees, their green canopies reclaiming the space. In the drawing, the factory was not a place of toil and despair but a backdrop to something new, something hopeful. The worker felt a lump rise in their throat as they watched their child, their small hands moving with purpose, their imagination unfettered by the realities that weighed so heavily on the adults around them. For the first time in years, the worker felt not just hope but possibility. Maybe, just maybe, the cycle could be broken.

Create a list of aspirations for children near, dear, & far below:

The night came as it always did, swallowing the town in a silence that felt oppressive rather than peaceful. Inside their small home, the woman prepared for her own shift, moving through the motions with a precision born not of routine but necessity. Her work was different from her partner's but no less grueling. While the factory roared with life during the day, her nights were spent in a quiet, almost ghostly room filled with rows of sewing machines, each one a sentinel of monotony and exhaustion. It was the kind of work that didn't leave visible scars but carved invisible ones into the soul, the kind of labor that reminded her at every moment of how little she mattered to the world she was keeping afloat.

The woman paused before leaving, looking at her sleeping child. Their face was soft and untroubled in the pale glow of the streetlight filtering through the window. It was in moments like this that she allowed herself to hope, to imagine that this endless grind was worth something, that her child might one day escape the weight of this life. But even as she hoped, a bitter voice in the back of her mind whispered doubts. She couldn't shield them from everything, the rising costs, the limited opportunities, the constant reminders that the world belonged to someone else. She smoothed the blanket over her child's small frame and turned away, steeling herself for the long night ahead.

The walk to the sewing shop was quiet but heavy, the air thick with a dampness that seemed to settle into her very bones. The streets were lined with darkened windows, the faint hum of distant traffic the only sound. She moved quickly, her footsteps echoing faintly on the cracked pavement, as though trying to outrun the thoughts that always surfaced on this journey. Why was it always like this? Why did it feel like the harder they worked, the less they had to show for it? The questions felt as endless as the shifts themselves, and the answers always seemed out of reach.

The sewing shop was a relic of a time when this town had seemed full of promise, when industries flourished, and families could make a living without sacrificing their health and dignity. Now, it was little more than a holding pen for those who had nowhere else to go, a place where labor was cheap and bodies were cheaper. The room was dimly lit, the machines arranged in neat rows that gave the impression of order even as they hummed with quiet desperation. The woman took her place at one of the machines, her hands moving almost mechanically as she guided fabric through the needle's relentless path. The soft whir of the machine was both soothing and maddening, a sound that had come to define her nights.

As she worked, her thoughts wandered to the newspapers she sometimes managed to glance at during brief moments of rest. They were filled with stories of economic recovery, of progress and prosperity, of opportunities that seemed to bloom everywhere except here. The headlines spoke of billionaires funding charitable projects, of industries innovating for a brighter future. They painted a picture so far removed from her reality that it felt like a cruel joke. She thought of the television ads she'd seen, the glossy images of smiling families, spacious homes, and endless possibilities. None of it felt real. None of it felt like it was meant for people like her.

The lies hurt as much as the reality. It wasn't just the physical exhaustion of her work or the financial strain of making ends meet. It was the gaslighting, the constant drumbeat of narratives that insisted things were better than they were, that people like her simply weren't trying hard enough. It was the knowledge that the world saw her not as a person but as a statistic, a number to be manipulated in a spreadsheet or a talking point in a speech. She thought of the phrase she'd read recently: "alternative facts." The term had enraged her, not because of its absurdity but because of its insidiousness. There were no alternative facts, only manufactured consent and propaganda designed to keep people like her in line.

The media's complicity in this charade was undeniable. The stories they chose to tell, the voices they amplified, the narratives they constructed, all of it served to protect the interests of the elite. The billionaires were framed as heroes, their greed disguised as ambition, their exploitation masked as generosity. The systems that crushed ordinary people were presented as inevitable, unchangeable. The woman thought about how often she had seen articles about "job creators," about the supposed virtues of trickle-down economics. She thought about how rarely, if ever, she'd seen stories about the workers who made those jobs possible, about the communities left behind when industries moved on, about the families struggling to survive in the shadows of wealth.

Her hands moved steadily as these thoughts swirled, the fabric flowing beneath the needle as though propelled by the weight of her anger. She thought about the lies she had been told her entire life, the promises that hard work would lead to success, that perseverance would be rewarded. She thought about the countless nights spent in this room, her body aching and her spirit fraying, while the world outside remained oblivious. And she thought about her child, whose future felt precariously balanced on the edge of a system determined to fail them.

The hours dragged on, each blending into the next in a blur of motion and fatigue. The woman's thoughts shifted to the other workers around her. They were a quiet, somber group, their faces marked by the same exhaustion she felt. She knew their stories in fragments, a mother trying to save enough to send her son to college, a man laid off from a better job years ago who had never recovered, a young woman whose eyes held a mixture of hope and fear that reminded her of her own child. They rarely spoke, the hum of the machines filling the silence, but their shared struggles created an unspoken bond. They were all fighting the same battle, even if they fought it alone.

The end of the shift came with relief immediately tempered by the knowledge that it would all begin again tomorrow. The woman gathered her things and stepped into the night, the air cooler now but no less heavy. She walked home slowly, her thoughts tangled in the web of frustration and despair that defined her existence. The streets were eerily quiet, a silence that felt like a void rather than a reprieve. How many people in this town were likely lying awake at this moment, their minds racing with the same worries that kept her up at night? How many felt as powerless as she did, as trapped by circumstances they couldn't control?

When she reached home, the house was dark except for the small lamp left on in the living room. She moved quietly, not wanting to disturb her sleeping family, but her thoughts refused to settle. She sat at the kitchen table, hands resting on its worn surface, and stared at the faint glow of the streetlight outside. She felt the weight of everything pressing down, the lies, the exhaustion, the relentless grind of a system designed to crush people like her. But she also felt something else, something small and fragile but undeniable. A spark of anger, not the kind that consumes but the kind that fuels. She thought about her child's drawings, about the dreams they still dared to have, and she felt a flicker of determination.

She knew she couldn't change the world on her own. The forces arrayed against her were vast and powerful, and the system was designed to resist change. But change had to start somewhere, and the cracks in the facade were growing larger every day. She thought about the other workers at the sewing shop, the people in her town, the countless others fighting the same fight. What might happen if they stopped believing the lies, stopped accepting the status quo, if they began to imagine something better?

As the first light of dawn began to filter through the window, the woman rose from the table. Her body ached, and her mind was still heavy with worry, but she felt a renewed sense of purpose. She looked at her sleeping child one last time before preparing to rest herself, knowing that the cycle would begin again soon. But this time, the thoughts that filled her mind were not just of despair but of possibility. She didn't have all the answers, but she had a

question that refused to be silenced: What if they could break the
cycle? What if they could rewrite the story?

The night had not brought peace, but it had brought clarity. The
lies and the gaslighting and the manufactured consent were tools
of control, but they could be resisted. The system that crushed her
could be challenged. And while the fight ahead would be long
and difficult, it was a fight worth waging. The woman lay down to
sleep, her thoughts still restless but her resolve quietly growing.
The night had ended, but the work was just beginning.

The Illusion of the Rock

The myth of meritocracy, so carefully constructed and perpetuated, finds its most damning refutation in the lives of those who labor endlessly yet remain entrenched in cycles of struggle. The factory worker, whose hands craft the profits of the wealthy, is not an exception, they are the rule. Their story is the story of countless others who toil under systems designed to extract their energy, their time, their very humanity, while rewarding them with just enough to survive. The factory is not just a place of work; it is a microcosm of the broader mechanisms of exploitation that define our economic reality. The worker's every movement, every ache and exhaustion, feeds a machine that exists solely to enrich those perched high above them, untouched by the sacrifices that sustain their wealth.

The billionaire class thrives on the illusion of meritocracy, using it as both shield and sword. They frame their wealth as the natural outcome of hard work and ingenuity, a reward for their supposed exceptionalism. But as we have seen, this narrative crumbles under scrutiny. Their success is not the product of merit but of systems rigged in their favor, systems that are upheld by policies, practices, and propaganda designed to keep workers in their place. Tax breaks, deregulation, subsidies, and lobbying are the tools of their ascendancy, not the mythical bootstrap they so often invoke. The factory worker's story, when viewed in the context of these systemic realities, becomes a damning indictment of the entire edifice of meritocracy.

Consider the disparity between the worker's life and the billionaire's. The worker labors through physical pain and emotional exhaustion, their dreams for their child tempered by the harsh realities of rising costs and stagnant wages. Their every effort contributes to the wealth of someone who remains invisible and untouchable, whose home is far removed from the grime and noise of the factory floor. The billionaire's life is one of unimaginable comfort, their wealth shielding them from the consequences of their actions. They do not feel the weight of student loans, the stress of choosing between rent and healthcare, or the despair of realizing that hard work is not enough to escape poverty. And yet, we are told that these billionaires deserve their wealth, that their success is proof of their merit. It is a lie so pervasive that it has become a cornerstone of our culture, shaping our perceptions of success and failure, of worth and value.

The policies that sustain this lie are not abstract; they are deeply personal. They manifest in the factory worker's inability to save for their child's education, in the mother's exhaustion after a night shift that barely covers the cost of groceries, in the quiet despair that settles over communities where opportunity has been systematically stripped away. These policies are the scaffolding of inequality, ensuring that wealth remains concentrated in the hands of the few while the many struggle to make ends meet. The tax code, for example, rewards those who hoard wealth, offering loopholes and deductions that are inaccessible to the average worker. Deregulation allows corporations to prioritize profit over safety, over sustainability, over human lives. Subsidies funnel public money into private hands, enriching the wealthy while leaving vital public services underfunded. Each of these mechanisms serves to deepen the chasm between the billionaire perched high on the rock and the workers struggling below.

The media, complicit in this system, plays a crucial role in maintaining the illusion. It tells us stories of self-made billionaires, of innovative disruptors, of philanthropic visionaries who supposedly elevate society with their wealth. But these stories are carefully curated, omitting the exploitation, the environmental degradation, and the systemic harm that underpins their fortunes. The media's focus on individual success obscures the collective struggles of workers, framing systemic issues as personal failings. It shifts the blame from the structures of inequality to the individuals who suffer under them, perpetuating the myth that poverty is a choice, that failure is a lack of effort, that the system itself is just.

The psychological toll of this gaslighting is profound. Workers are not only burdened by the material realities of their lives but also by the constant message that their struggles are their own fault. They are told that if they work harder, if they make better choices, if they simply try more, they too can succeed. This narrative isolates and demoralizes, turning systemic oppression into a personal failing. It prevents solidarity, replacing collective action with individual striving, and ensures that the cycle of exploitation remains unbroken. But beneath this manufactured despair lies a truth that cannot be erased: the power of the billionaire class is not absolute. It is fragile, dependent on the very workers it seeks to oppress. And once that truth is recognized, the illusion begins to crumble.

As we close this chapter, let us turn back to the image of the otter perched high on a rock, gazing down at the smaller otters struggling in the shallow waters below. This visual is not just a metaphor; it is a mirror held up to our society. The otter on the rock represents the billionaire, elevated not by their own merit but by the labor and sacrifices of those below. The smaller otters, their movements frantic as they search for sustenance, are the workers, the many who sustain the few. The rock itself is the system, a structure designed to maintain the distance between those who have and those who have not. It is a stark and sobering image, one that captures the unequal distribution of resources and opportunities that defines our world.

But the image also holds a seed of hope. The waters below the rock are not static; they are alive with movement, with potential. The smaller otters, though struggling, are not powerless. They are many, and their collective strength has the power to reshape the landscape. The rock, though imposing, is not unassailable. It can be eroded, dismantled, brought down by the force of the rising tide. And that tide is rising. The waters are moving, and change is coming.

Chapter 2
Trickle Down Tyranny

The lie of trickle-down economics is one of the most enduring and destructive myths of modern capitalism. It is a story told by the powerful to justify their wealth, a narrative that claims that by allowing resources to flow freely to the top, they will inevitably trickle down to everyone else. This idea has been sold to the public as common sense, as the natural order of things, but in practice, it has been nothing more than a smokescreen for policies designed to funnel wealth upward while leaving the majority to fight over the scraps. Trickle-down economics is not a failure of theory, it is a strategy of control, a deliberate mechanism to entrench inequality and protect the billionaire class at all costs.

At its core, trickle-down economics is based on the premise that wealth at the top creates opportunities for those at the bottom. We are told that when billionaires thrive, everyone benefits, that their investments create jobs, their innovations drive progress, and their success fuels economic growth. But history tells a very different story. Time and again, we have seen that the wealth accumulated by the few does not trickle down, it pools at the top, hoarded and protected by systems designed to ensure its permanence. The promises of prosperity for all have turned into realities of stagnation and decline for the many. Trickle-down economics is not a rising tide that lifts all boats; it is a siphon that drains resources from the majority to enrich the few.

The failures of this theory are not abstract; they are written into the lived experiences of millions. Consider the tax cuts sold as economic stimulants, designed to incentivize investment and job creation. These cuts overwhelmingly benefit the wealthy, allowing billionaires and corporations to pocket billions while contributing little to the communities they claim to serve. Meanwhile, the public services that working people rely on, schools, healthcare, infrastructure, are left underfunded, their budgets slashed in the name of fiscal responsibility. The result is a society where the wealthy build their empires on tax breaks and subsidies while the working class bears the brunt of austerity measures and rising costs.

Take, for example, the manufacturing industry. Decades of deregulation and globalization, justified under the guise of economic efficiency, have decimated industrial towns and left millions of workers displaced. Factories once provided stable jobs and decent wages, anchoring communities and offering a path to the middle class. But as corporations chased cheaper labor abroad and prioritized shareholder profits over worker welfare, these jobs disappeared. The workers who built these industries were left behind, their communities hollowed out and their futures uncertain. And yet, the billionaire owners of these corporations thrived, their fortunes growing even as their employees faced unemployment and poverty. Trickle-down economics has not created opportunities for these workers; it has created billionaires at their expense.

The tech industry provides another stark example. We are told that technology is a force for progress, that the wealth generated by tech billionaires represents the future of innovation. But beneath the glossy narratives of disruption and entrepreneurship lies a reality of exploitation and inequality. The gig economy, heralded as a model of flexibility and freedom, has turned millions of workers into independent contractors with no benefits, no protections, and no stability. Tech giants rake in billions while their drivers, delivery workers, and content moderators struggle to make a living. The promise of trickle-down wealth has left these workers scrambling for survival, their labor undervalued and their dignity ignored.

This system is not maintained by accident; it is upheld by deliberate choices made by policymakers. Laws, tax codes, and subsidies are crafted with the input of lobbyists and corporate donors, ensuring that the billionaire class remains protected while the working class is left vulnerable. Campaign contributions buy influence, shaping policies that prioritize the interests of the wealthy over the needs of the majority. Billionaires use their wealth to fund think tanks, media outlets, and political campaigns that perpetuate the myth of trickle-down economics, creating an ecosystem of propaganda that shields them from accountability.

56

They shape public opinion, framing their wealth as a benefit to society rather than a symptom of systemic injustice.

The media plays a crucial role in this ecosystem, amplifying the narratives that protect the billionaire class. Stories of entrepreneurial success dominate headlines, presenting billionaires as self-made heroes who earned their fortunes through ingenuity and hard work. The media rarely interrogates the systemic forces that enabled their rise, nor does it highlight the harm caused by their wealth accumulation. Instead, it celebrates their philanthropy, casting them as benevolent figures whose charitable donations are framed as acts of generosity rather than tools of power. This narrative obscures the reality that their wealth was built on the backs of workers whose struggles are rarely, if ever, acknowledged.

The tactics used to maintain this system are not just about protecting wealth; they are about suppressing opposition. Billionaires fund campaigns that pit workers against one another, using divisions of race, class, and geography to prevent solidarity. They invest in narratives that blame individuals for systemic failures, telling us that poverty is the result of laziness, that success is a matter of effort, and that inequality is the price of progress. These narratives are weapons, wielded to keep us compliant, to ensure that we do not question the structures that perpetuate inequality.

The human cost of these policies and narratives is staggering. The factory worker who loses their job to outsourcing, the single mother who can't afford childcare, the gig worker who drives long hours for barely enough to get by, these are not isolated stories; they are the lived realities of millions. Trickle-down economics has left a trail of despair and disillusionment, creating a society where wealth is concentrated at the top while the majority are left to fend for themselves. The promises of prosperity have turned into the realities of precarity, and the gap between the haves and the have-nots has become a chasm that feels impossible to bridge.

The promise of technology has always been to make our lives easier, to grant us more time and resources to pursue happiness, creativity, and connection. Yet, in this era of unprecedented technological advancement, we find ourselves not liberated but further entangled in the webs of exploitation and control. The digital age has made us more productive than ever before. Tasks that once required hours or days are now completed in minutes, and yet the rewards of this productivity have not been shared equitably. Instead, they have been hoarded by the billionaire class, who have turned the tools of progress into instruments of domination.

At the heart of this exploitation is the commodification of our lives. The promise of technology was that it would free us, but instead, it has made us the product. Every search, every click, every interaction is harvested, analyzed, and monetized without our consent. Our data, the digital footprints of our daily lives, has become a resource more valuable than oil, and yet we receive nothing for it. Social media platforms, search engines, and online retailers profit from our information, building immense fortunes while we are left with invasive ads, shrinking privacy, and the growing sense that we are losing control of our own lives. This is not innovation; it is theft, a new frontier in the extraction of wealth and power.

Consider how artificial intelligence (AI) and machine learning, heralded as the next great revolution, have been weaponized against us. These technologies could be used to enhance our lives, to automate drudgery, and to open up new possibilities for creativity and connection. Instead, they are used to surveil us, to manipulate our behavior, and to maximize profits for corporations. AI algorithms decide what news we see, what products are marketed to us, and even how much we pay for goods and services. These systems are not neutral; they are designed to serve the interests of the powerful, perpetuating inequality and eroding our autonomy. They track our movements, predict our desires, and nudge us toward choices that benefit corporations at the expense of our well-being.

Blockchain technology, with its potential to decentralize power and democratize access to wealth, has similarly been co-opted. Originally envisioned as a tool to empower individuals and bypass corrupt institutions, blockchain has been overshadowed by the rise of scam cryptocurrencies and speculative markets that enrich a select few while leaving the majority disillusioned. The ideals of decentralization and transparency have been drowned out by the noise of get-rich-quick schemes and the consolidation of power among a new class of tech elites. True decentralized currencies like Bitcoin, when used responsibly, offer a glimpse of what could be: systems that return control to the people, that operate outside the grip of central banks and financial oligarchs. But instead of realizing this vision, we find ourselves in a digital economy that mirrors the inequalities of the old system, with billionaires profiting while the rest of us are left to navigate a landscape of scams and volatility.

The consequences of this technological betrayal are profound. We are not only more productive but also more surveilled, more manipulated, and more alienated than ever before. The gig economy, powered by digital platforms, exemplifies this dynamic. Companies like Uber, DoorDash, and Amazon Mechanical Turk promise flexibility and freedom but deliver precarity and exploitation. Workers are treated as disposable, their labor reduced to data points in algorithms that optimize for corporate profit. These platforms profit from the labor of millions while evading the responsibilities that come with traditional employment. Benefits, protections, and stability are stripped away, leaving workers to bear the risks while corporations reap the rewards.

The erosion of privacy is another critical aspect of this technological dystopia. Every device, every app, every online service collects data, creating a digital portrait of our lives that is far more intimate than we might realize. This data is not only sold to advertisers but also used to predict and influence our behavior. It shapes the content we see, the prices we pay, and even the opportunities available to us. The loss of privacy is not just an inconvenience; it is a fundamental shift in power, a transfer of control from individuals to corporations and governments. When our lives are laid bare to those who profit from our vulnerabilities, we lose more than privacy, we lose autonomy, agency, and dignity.

Yet, even as we grapple with these challenges, the potential of technology remains immense. AI, blockchain, and decentralized systems have the power to transform our society for the better, to create a world where wealth is shared, where power is distributed, and where individuals have greater control over their lives. Imagine an AI designed to serve the public good, to enhance education, healthcare, and civic engagement rather than corporate profits. Imagine a blockchain-based economy where transparency and accountability are the norm, where corruption and exploitation are no longer viable strategies. These technologies could empower communities, amplify voices, and foster collaboration on a scale never before possible.

But to realize this potential, we must confront the systems that have turned technology into a tool of oppression. The billionaire class has harnessed these advancements to entrench their power, to extract ever more wealth from the rest of us, and to stifle the transformative possibilities of these tools. They have turned innovation into a weapon, using it to consolidate their dominance rather than to uplift humanity. This is not an inevitable outcome; it is a choice, one that reflects the priorities of those who hold power.

The path forward requires us to reclaim technology, to wrest it from the hands of the few and make it work for the many. This means demanding greater accountability from tech companies, pushing for policies that protect privacy and labor rights, and investing in public initiatives that harness technology for the common good. It means challenging the narratives that frame surveillance and exploitation as the price of progress, and instead imagining a future where technology serves as a tool of liberation rather than control.

The human cost of our current trajectory is too high to ignore. The erosion of wages, the loss of privacy, the commodification of our lives, these are not abstract issues; they are realities that shape our daily existence. But the same tools that have been used to exploit us can also be used to empower us. Decentralized networks, open-source platforms, and cooperative models offer a glimpse of what is possible when technology is aligned with the values of equity and justice. These are not utopian fantasies; they are practical solutions that challenge the dominance of the billionaire class and put power back into the hands of the people.

Wrestling Control Back: Building Tools for Liberation

The first step in wrestling control back from the forces that exploit us is recognizing the power we already possess. The billionaires who dominate our economy and culture rely on our compliance. They depend on our continued use of their platforms, our willingness to trade our data for convenience, and our acceptance of their narratives. To fight back, we must begin to withdraw our consent. This means breaking free from the systems they have designed to keep us distracted, divided, and disempowered. It starts with rejecting the poison of unsocial apps and reclaiming our time, attention, and creativity for purposes that serve the common good.

Social media platforms have become the playgrounds of exploitation. Designed to be addictive, these apps manipulate our emotions, harvest our data, and sell our attention to the highest bidder. They foster division and outrage, keeping us locked in cycles of distraction and despair. The first step for anyone, coder, student, or activist, is to unplug from these systems. Encourage kids to reduce their screen time, to spend less time scrolling through curated fantasies and more time engaging with the world around them. Help them see the apps for what they are: tools of control masquerading as tools of connection. The moment we reclaim our time from these platforms is the moment we begin to reclaim our agency.

But rejecting the tools of exploitation is only the beginning. The real fight lies in creating alternatives. Coders, engineers, and innovators have an incredible opportunity, and responsibility, to build the next generation of tools that empower rather than exploit. Imagine platforms that prioritize community over profit, tools that protect privacy rather than invading it, and systems that distribute power instead of concentrating it. These are not pipe dreams; they are entirely achievable if we shift our focus away from the profit-driven models that dominate today's tech landscape.

One way to encourage this shift is by fostering a culture of open-source collaboration. The open-source movement has already shown us the potential of collective innovation. By sharing knowledge and resources, coders can build tools that are transparent, accountable, and accessible to everyone. Encourage young people to learn programming languages, to contribute to open-source projects, and to see coding not as a path to personal wealth but as a way to solve problems and serve communities. Highlight examples of successful open-source initiatives, from the Linux operating system to decentralized communication tools, to show what is possible when profit is not the primary motive.

Education is key. Schools and communities should prioritize teaching coding and digital literacy as essential skills, alongside critical thinking and media literacy. Kids need to understand not only how to use technology but also how it works, how it shapes their lives, and how they can shape it in return. Encourage them to question the tools they use, to ask who benefits from them, and to imagine how they could be redesigned to benefit everyone. Empower them to see themselves not as passive consumers but as active creators, capable of building the future they want to live in.

We must also address the cultural narratives that glorify tech billionaires and their exploitative systems. Young people are often taught to admire figures like Elon Musk and Mark Zuckerberg, seeing them as geniuses who changed the world. But these narratives obscure the harm caused by their business practices and the systemic inequalities they perpetuate. Teach kids to look beyond the surface, to see the labor and exploitation that underpin these empires, and to value collective achievements over individual wealth. Celebrate the unsung heroes of technology, the teachers, the researchers, the community organizers, who work tirelessly to create tools and systems that truly serve the public good.

To wrest control back, we also need to build and invest in decentralized technologies. Blockchain, when used ethically, offers a model for systems that operate without centralized control. Encourage coders to explore the potential of decentralized platforms, currencies, and applications that return power to individuals and communities. For example, imagine a social network that is not owned by a corporation but by its users, where data is not harvested but protected. Or consider decentralized energy grids that empower communities to generate and share renewable energy locally. These technologies exist; they need only the right minds and motivations to flourish.

Another critical step is creating incentives for innovation that prioritizes people and the planet. Governments, educational institutions, and nonprofit organizations can play a vital role by funding projects that align with values of equity, sustainability, and community empowerment. Hackathons, competitions, and grants can encourage young coders to focus on solving real-world problems rather than chasing the next viral app. Recognize and reward projects that address issues like climate change, access to education, and economic inequality. By shifting the focus from profit to purpose, we can inspire a new generation of innovators to build tools that truly matter.

Encouraging collaboration between disciplines is also essential. The challenges we face are complex, requiring insights from diverse fields. Coders should work alongside educators, environmentalists, sociologists, and activists to ensure that the tools they create address the full scope of human and environmental needs. Break down the silos that often isolate tech from other areas of knowledge, and foster a spirit of interdisciplinary problem-solving. This approach not only leads to better solutions but also reinforces the idea that technology should serve society, not dominate it.

Finally, we must cultivate a sense of urgency and possibility. The problems we face, climate change, inequality, the erosion of privacy, are immense, but they are not insurmountable. Show kids and coders that they have the power to make a difference, that their skills and creativity are not just valuable but essential. Remind them that every tool they build, every idea they share, every step they take toward reclaiming control is part of a larger movement to create a better world.

The time to act is now. The tools of exploitation that dominate our lives did not emerge overnight; they were built, piece by piece, by individuals and institutions with clear goals and motives.

We can build new tools with the same intentionality, tools that reflect our values and aspirations rather than our fears and divisions. This is not just a technological challenge; it is a moral and societal one. It requires all of us to reject complacency, to question the systems that shape our lives, and to imagine and create the world we want to live in.

In the end, the goal is to redefine what control means. It is not about domination but empowerment, not about profit but purpose. It is about creating systems that uplift everyone, that prioritize humanity and the planet over greed and power. The next generation of tools is waiting to be built. Let's give them the knowledge, and the encouragement they need and want.

20 Actionable Technology Steps & Examples

Unplug from exploitative platforms – Set aside dedicated time each day to disconnect from social media and instead focus on creative, educational, or community-driven activities.

Learn coding skills – Encourage children and adults alike to start with free coding platforms like Codecademy, Khan Academy, or freeCodeCamp to gain programming skills.

Contribute to open-source projects – Join platforms like GitHub to collaborate on projects that serve the public good, such as privacy-focused browsers or secure messaging apps.

Develop alternatives to exploitative systems – Create decentralized, user-owned platforms that prioritize transparency and equity, such as Mastodon for social networking.

Host hackathons for social good – Organize local or virtual hackathons to tackle problems like access to clean water, affordable housing, or renewable energy solutions.

Start community education programs – Launch workshops in schools, libraries, or community centers to teach digital literacy and critical thinking about technology.

Build apps for underserved communities – Design tools for improving access to resources, like apps that connect people with food banks or affordable healthcare.

Support decentralized currency (Bitcoin) responsibly – Educate communities on legitimate blockchain applications like Bitcoin and how they challenge centralized financial systems.

Invest in renewable energy tech – Develop or promote open-source solar panel designs or neighborhood energy-sharing programs using blockchain.

Create privacy-first tools – Build apps and browsers that emphasize user privacy, such as Brave, DuckDuckGo, or Signal, to protect people from data exploitation.

Collaborate across disciplines – Partner coders with sociologists, educators, or environmental scientists to create tools that address multifaceted societal problems.

Promote responsible AI use – Develop ethical AI tools that focus on improving public education, healthcare, or climate solutions instead of maximizing corporate profit.

Launch grassroots tech cooperatives – Organize community-owned tech platforms where members share in the decision-making and profits.

Develop educational games – Design interactive apps or games that teach children about critical thinking, sustainability, or technology's impact on society.

Build public-access Wi-Fi networks – Create secure and equitable internet access points in underserved areas to reduce the digital divide.

Use technology to fight misinformation – Develop tools to detect and debunk fake news for informed civic engagement.

Encourage kids to create, not consume – Provide resources and mentorship for young people to design their own websites, apps, or games with purpose.

Advocate for tech accountability laws – For policies that hold corporations accountable for data misuse exploitations.

Design tools for digital activism – Build apps that facilitate organizing, fundraising, or petitioning for social causes.

Foster a culture of repair and reuse – Promote initiatives that teach hardware repair and software reuse to reduce e-waste and dependency on large tech corporations.

Create a list of your particular skill set to fight greed below:

A Town Left Behind

The streets of the town lay unnaturally quiet, a stillness that spoke of something lost, something stolen. The factory, once the heart of this community, now stood as a hollowed-out monument to betrayal. Its gates were chained shut, the windows darkened, and the air around it felt heavier, as if even the wind knew better than to disturb this place of ruin. The displaced worker walked those empty streets, their footsteps echoing faintly against the rows of shuttered shops and boarded-up homes. Every corner of this town bore the scars of the factory's closure, a gas station with "For Sale" signs flapping in the breeze, a diner that had once buzzed with the laughter of shift workers now silent, its chairs stacked neatly on tables as if waiting for a return that would never come.

This worker, whose hands had once built the products that made the factory owner rich, now carried nothing but a plastic bag filled with the few groceries they could still afford. Their face, lined with exhaustion, was a map of grief and resilience. They passed familiar landmarks, the park where their child had once played, the school that now struggled to keep its doors open. Each step reminded them of what had been taken, not just from them but from everyone in this town. The factory's closure was not just a business decision; it was a severing, a wound that had left the community bleeding. The worker thought of their child, who had grown quieter in recent months, their once-bright questions about the world replaced by a sullen acceptance that the answers would not come.

At the center of the town square, the worker paused, looking up at the statue of a long-forgotten industrialist who had built the factory decades ago. The plaque at its base proclaimed, "To Progress and Prosperity," words that now felt like a cruel joke. Progress for whom? Prosperity for whom? Certainly not for the families who had given their lives to that factory, only to be discarded when profits demanded it. The worker's gaze lingered on the statue, their thoughts heavy with questions they didn't yet have the words to articulate. They turned away and continued walking, their bag of groceries swinging lightly at their side, a small and bitter reminder of what remained.

Across town, the same story repeated itself in different variations. The shopkeeper, whose store had once been a gathering place for the community, now sat alone behind the counter, flipping through invoices they knew they couldn't pay. The shelves were half-empty, the aisles deserted. The shopkeeper's hands shook slightly as they traced the edges of an eviction notice, their mind racing with impossible calculations. They thought of the factory workers who had once filled this store, their laughter and banter echoing through the aisles as they bought supplies for their families. Without them, the store was just another hollow shell, a place that had lost its purpose.

At the school, a teacher sat in a dimly lit classroom, staring at a stack of lesson plans they couldn't bring themselves to finish. The budget cuts had come swiftly after the factory's closure, leaving them with fewer resources and more students in need. The teacher thought about the children in their care, so many of whom had stopped turning in assignments or showing up at all. They thought of the teenager in the back row, the one whose father had worked at the factory for thirty years, who now sat silently through class, their eyes distant, their mind clearly elsewhere. The teacher felt a pang of helplessness, a deep ache for all the futures that seemed to be slipping away.

The teenager, walking home from school that day, felt the weight of everything in ways they couldn't yet fully articulate. They passed the empty factory, its gates now overgrown with weeds, and felt a strange mix of anger and curiosity. They thought about their family, about the long nights spent around the kitchen table trying to stretch too little money too far. They thought about the factory owner, whose name was still spoken in hushed tones around town, as though saying it too loudly might summon some new misfortune. They had seen pictures of his mansion on the news once, a sprawling estate with perfectly manicured lawns and shimmering pools. It was a world so far removed from their own that it might as well have been a different planet.

The teenager's curiosity turned to anger as they thought about that mansion, about the wealth that had been built on their father's labor and their mother's sacrifices. They didn't yet have the vocabulary to name it, greed, exploitation, systemic injustice, but they felt it all the same, a sharp, burning sense of wrongness that refused to be ignored. They had started asking questions, not just to their parents but to anyone who would listen. Why did the factory close? Why did the owner get to keep his wealth while the town suffered? Why was this happening, and who had decided that it was acceptable? The answers they received were often vague or resigned, but the questions kept coming, each one sharpening their awareness.

The voices of the displaced workers blended together in a chorus of despair and quiet fury. There was the young parent who spoke of standing in line at the food bank, their child clutching their leg and asking why they couldn't have the same snacks as their friends at school. There was the retiree whose pension had vanished when the factory closed, leaving them to choose between heat in the winter and medication for their chronic illness. There was the former supervisor who had believed in the promises of the factory owner, who had encouraged their team to work harder, only to be cast aside like everyone else. Each voice added to the mosaic of loss, each story a piece of a larger picture that was becoming increasingly clear.

As the teenager listened to these stories, they began to see the patterns that tied them all together. This wasn't just about the factory; it was about a system that prioritized profit over people, that treated workers as expendable and communities as collateral damage. They thought about the factory owner, whose wealth remained untouched by the closure, who had likely moved on to some new venture without a second thought for the lives left in his wake. The teenager's anger grew, but so did their determination. They began to see that their family's struggles were not isolated incidents but part of a larger system designed to exploit and discard.

The narrative of the town's collapse culminated in a quiet but powerful moment of reflection. The displaced workers gathered at the community center, a space that had once hosted celebrations and town meetings but now felt like a refuge for the wounded. They shared their stories, their frustrations, and their fears. But as they spoke, something shifted. The despair that had weighed so heavily on them began to give way to a simmering anger, a collective realization that their suffering was not inevitable. They started to see their struggles not as individual failures but as evidence of a system that had failed them.

The teenager, sitting at the edge of the room, watched and listened. For the first time, they saw their community not as a collection of isolated tragedies but as a group of people bound together by shared pain and a growing sense of injustice. They felt the first flickers of something new, something they couldn't yet name but knew was important. It was a glimmer of opposition, a faint but persistent hope that things could be different. And in that moment, the teenager began to imagine what it might look like to fight back.

The community center, dimly lit and worn from years of use, had become a gathering place for the displaced workers and their families. The air inside was thick with a mixture of frustration and exhaustion, voices mingling as people shared their stories of what the factory's closure had taken from them. The space, once a hub for birthday parties and town meetings, now felt heavy with a new purpose, not celebration, but survival. The teenager, sitting quietly near the back of the room, listened as the stories flowed, each one adding another thread to the tapestry of loss that was now their town.

An older man, once a machine operator at the factory, stood to speak. His voice, roughened by decades of shouting over the roar of equipment, carried a weight that silenced the room. "I've worked since I was sixteen," he said, his hands trembling slightly as he gripped the back of a chair. "I gave everything to that place. My back, my health, my time. And what did it get me? Not even a phone call when they shut the gates." He paused, looking around the room, his gaze landing on the teenager for a moment before continuing. "We built that factory. It was ours. But they took it from us like it was nothing."

Another voice cut in, this one belonging to a woman who had run the diner down the street from the factory. "It's not just the jobs," she said, her voice tight with anger. "It's everything else. When the factory went, so did the customers. I had to close my doors last week. Thirty years I've been there. Now I don't know how

I'm going to pay the mortgage." Her words hung in the air, the quiet murmurs of agreement from the others only amplifying the gravity of her situation.

The teenager shifted in their seat, taking in the stories with a mixture of anger and unease. They had heard these things before, in fragments, at home, at school, in passing conversations, but here, in this room, the weight of it all felt undeniable. These weren't just isolated tragedies; they were pieces of a larger pattern, a system that seemed designed to crush people like their family and neighbors. And yet, as the voices continued to rise and fall, a new feeling began to take root in the teenager's chest, a flicker of determination, small but steady.

The room grew quieter as a younger man began to speak. He was a former foreman, someone who had once believed in the promises of the factory's owner. "I used to tell my team to give it their all," he said, his voice tinged with regret. "I told them that hard work would pay off, that the company would take care of us if we took care of it. But that wasn't true, was it? They didn't care about us. They cared about their profits. And when it wasn't enough for them, they left us with nothing." He shook his head, his shoulders slumping. "I should've seen it coming. We all should've seen it coming."

The teenager felt a surge of anger at those words, not directed at the foreman but at the system he was describing. How had it been allowed to happen? How could people work so hard, give so much, and be discarded so easily? Their mind raced with questions, each one sharpening the edges of their frustration. They thought about the factory owner, who had likely moved on to some new venture, untouched by the devastation he'd left behind. They thought about the mansion they'd seen in the news, the sprawling estate that stood in stark contrast to the boarded-up homes and empty streets of their town. The unfairness of it all felt overwhelming.

As the meeting continued, the teenager's thoughts began to shift. The despair and anger in the room were palpable, but there was something else, too, a sense of shared purpose, a recognition that their struggles were not individual but collective. They listened more closely, trying to piece together the threads of what was being said. The older man talked about how the union had once fought for better conditions, how solidarity had been their greatest weapon against the factory's demands. The diner owner spoke of how the town had come together during tough times in the past, supporting one another when it felt like the world had turned its back on them. Even the foreman, who had once believed in the promises of the factory, seemed to be searching for a way to make amends.

The teenager's mind began to race with possibilities. What if the town could come together again? What if they could find a way to fight back, to reclaim what had been taken from them? They didn't know exactly how, but the idea refused to let go. They thought about their friends at school, many of whom had parents who had also worked at the factory. They thought about the teachers who were struggling to keep the school running despite shrinking budgets. They thought about their own family, about the long nights spent worrying about bills and food and the future. And they thought about the factory owner, whose name had become synonymous with greed and betrayal in their mind. The teenager clenched their fists, a spark of resolve flickering in their chest.

The meeting began to wind down, the voices fading into a quiet murmur as people prepared to leave. The teenager's parents stood, exchanging tired but hopeful words with their neighbors. The teenager followed them out into the cool night air, their thoughts still racing. The streets were dark and empty, the silence broken only by the faint rustling of leaves in the breeze. But for the first time in months, the teenager didn't feel entirely hopeless. The stories they had heard, the anger and determination in that room, had sparked something in them. It wasn't just despair anymore; it was the beginning of something else, something they couldn't yet name but knew was important.

As they walked home, the teenager glanced back at the community center, its windows glowing softly in the darkness. They thought about what had been said inside, about the shared pain and the faint glimmers of opposition that had begun to emerge. They didn't know what the future held, but they knew one thing for certain: they weren't alone. And that, for now, was enough to keep them moving forward.

The days that followed were filled with small but significant changes. The teenager began to ask more questions, not just of their parents but of their teachers, their friends, and even themselves. They started reading about the history of labor movements, about how ordinary people had fought back against systems that seemed unchangeable. They began to see their town not as a place of defeat but as a place of possibility, a community that could rise from its struggles if it found a way to come together.

At school, the teenager began to share what they had learned, planting seeds of curiosity and determination in their peers. They talked about what they had heard at the community center, about the stories of loss and resilience, about the idea that their struggles were part of something bigger. Some of their classmates listened with interest, while others dismissed their words with shrugs or skepticism. But the teenager didn't let that deter them. They kept talking, kept questioning, kept imagining what might be possible if they all stood together.

Back at the community center, the displaced workers continued to meet, their conversations growing more focused and determined. They began to talk not just about what had been lost but about what could be done. They discussed the possibility of organizing, of demanding accountability from the factory owner and the systems that had enabled him. They talked about starting small businesses, about pooling their resources to create new opportunities for the town. The teenager listened closely, their mind buzzing with ideas and possibilities.

One evening, as the sun set over the town, the teenager stood at the edge of the empty factory gates, staring at the overgrown weeds and rusting metal. They thought about everything they had learned in the past weeks, about the stories they had heard and the resolve they had seen in their neighbors. They thought about the future, about the kind of world they wanted to build, not just for themselves but for everyone in their community. And as the first stars appeared in the sky, the teenager made a silent promise:

they would not let this be the end. They would fight for their town, for their family, for a future where no one had to suffer the way their community had. It was just a beginning, but it was a beginning that mattered.

Synthesis and the Stream's Truth

The closure of the factory was not an isolated tragedy; it was a symptom of a far larger disease. This was not a natural disaster, not an unavoidable consequence of progress. It was a deliberate act, orchestrated by a system that prioritizes profit over people, consolidation over community, and greed over justice. The billionaire who owned the factory did not close its doors because he had to. He closed them because the rules of our economy rewarded him for doing so. In a world built on trickle-down economics, decisions like these are not anomalies, they are the intended outcome.

Trickle-down economics has always been a lie, a myth sold to the public to justify policies that funnel wealth upward and leave communities like this one to wither. The logic is simple but deeply flawed: let the rich grow richer, and their wealth will eventually benefit everyone else. But in practice, the only thing that trickles down is despair. Tax cuts for corporations do not create jobs; they create stock buybacks. Deregulation does not spur innovation; it paves the way for exploitation. Subsidies for billion-dollar industries do not uplift communities; they line the pockets of those who already have more than they could ever need.

The factory's closure is a textbook example of how this system operates. For decades, the workers of this town gave their labor, their time, and their health to build the wealth of someone they would never meet. In return, they were promised stability, fair wages, and the chance to build a better future for their families. But those promises were hollow, and when the time came for the factory owner to choose between his profits and the people who had made them possible, he chose the former without hesitation. The policies that allowed him to make this choice, and profit from it, were not accidents. They were the result of deliberate decisions by policymakers who serve the interests of the wealthy.

The mechanisms that uphold this system are insidious and pervasive. Lobbying ensures that laws are written to benefit corporations and billionaires, not workers or communities. Campaign financing allows the wealthy to buy influence, shaping policy in their favor while the voices of ordinary people are drowned out. The media, owned by the same billionaires who profit from these systems, perpetuates narratives that justify inequality and obscure its human cost. Stories of self-made billionaires dominate headlines, while the struggles of workers are ignored or dismissed. This is not just about money; it is about power, about control, about ensuring that the system remains rigged in favor of the few at the expense of the many.

The human cost of this rigged system is staggering. The factory's closure did not just take away jobs; it took away a sense of purpose, of stability, of belonging. It hollowed out a community, leaving behind empty streets, boarded-up businesses, and families struggling to survive. The ripple effects are felt in every corner of the town, in the school where teachers stretch dwindling resources, in the food bank where lines grow longer by the day, in the homes where parents lie awake at night wondering how they will make it to the next paycheck. These are not isolated stories; they are the lived realities of millions across the country, communities abandoned by a system that sees them as expendable.

But this story is not just about despair. It is also about recognition, about understanding that this system is not inevitable. The suffering of this town is not the result of natural laws or market forces; it is the result of choices. Choices made by billionaires who prioritize their wealth over humanity. Choices made by politicians who cater to the interests of the wealthy while ignoring the needs of their constituents. Choices made by a society that has allowed itself to be seduced by the myth of trickle-down economics. And just as these choices were made, they can be unmade. The system is not immutable; it can be challenged, dismantled, and rebuilt.

As we return to the image of the otters in the stream, the metaphor becomes clear. The otter perched high on the rock, gazing down at those struggling in the shallow waters below, represents the billionaire class. Their position is not natural; it is constructed. The rock they stand on is built from the labor and sacrifices of those below, from the resources siphoned away from communities like this one. The otters in the stream, their movements frantic as they search for sustenance, represent the workers, the families, the communities left to fend for themselves. The water, reduced to a trickle, symbolizes the resources that have been hoarded, the opportunities that have been stolen.

But the stream also holds a truth that cannot be ignored. Water, no matter how diminished, has the power to erode even the tallest rock. The otters below are not powerless. Their struggle, their resilience, their refusal to give up, these are the forces that can reshape the landscape. The billionaire may sit high on his rock today, but he is not untouchable. The rock is not unassailable. The waters are rising, and with them, the possibility of change. The key to this change lies in recognizing the power of the collective. The people of this town, like so many others, have been told that their struggles are individual failures, that their suffering is the result of personal shortcomings rather than systemic injustice. But as they gather in the community center, as they share their stories and their anger, they begin to see the truth. Their struggles are not isolated; they are interconnected. Their pain is not the result of their own failings; it is the result of a system that has failed them.

Opposition does not begin with grand gestures or sweeping revolutions. It begins with small acts of defiance, with the decision to question the narratives that have been imposed upon us. It begins with conversations in community centers, with teenagers asking hard questions, with workers refusing to accept the status quo. It begins with recognizing that the system is not natural or inevitable; it is constructed, and what is constructed can be dismantled.

Chapter 3
A Vision of Technofeudalism

The billionaires of today no longer care whether we like them. The veneer of philanthropy, once used to soften the glaring inequality of their wealth, has been discarded. They no longer pretend to serve the greater good or maintain even the illusion of social responsibility. Figures like Curtis Yarvin, with their unabashed embrace of technofeudalism, reveal a new ambition for humanity, one where the few reign as untouchable overlords and the masses exist solely to serve their interests as serfs.* This is not just a continuation of capitalism; it is a mutation, a system designed to strip humanity of its dignity and autonomy, replacing the pretense of democracy with the cold efficiency of control.

The vision is dystopian in every sense of the word. Imagine a world where algorithms determine your worth, where your every move is tracked, analyzed, and monetized. In this society, there is no upward mobility, no escape from the roles assigned to you by an invisible digital hand. You are not a citizen; you are a data point, a product to be optimized for profit. The billionaires at the helm of this system do not see themselves as part of the same humanity they exploit. They see themselves as something apart, something superior. Their wealth, they believe, is proof of their inherent superiority, their right to rule.

This shift in ambition is evident in the industries and technologies they champion. No longer content with owning land, resources, or businesses, they now seek to own the very fabric of our lives. They invest in technologies that extend their control, surveillance systems that monitor every aspect of public and private life, artificial intelligence that replaces human decision-making, and digital platforms that dictate the flow of information. These tools are not used to empower or liberate; they are used to enforce compliance, to ensure that the masses remain docile and dependent.

Curtis Yarvin's ideology exemplifies this new vision. His concept of technofeudalism imagines a society where traditional democratic structures are obsolete, replaced by corporate-run city-states and authoritarian rule. It is a vision that dismisses the idea of equality as naive, that sees power and control as the natural order of things. In Yarvin's world, billionaires are not just wealthy; they are sovereigns, rulers of their own domains, free from the constraints of accountability or morality. This is the world they are building, brick by digital brick.

The ideology underpinning technofeudalism is not subtle. It is a direct assault on democracy and human dignity. It seeks to reduce people to their economic utility, stripping away the rights and freedoms that have been fought for over centuries. In this vision, the masses are not citizens but subjects, their lives dictated by the whims of those who hold the reins of technology. The billionaire class has no interest in fostering a society of equals; their goal is to create a society of servants, a digital serfdom where their power is absolute.

Technology, once heralded as a tool for liberation, has been weaponized to enforce this vision. Algorithms designed to optimize efficiency are now used to optimize control. Surveillance systems, initially justified as tools for security, have become instruments of oppression. Social media platforms, which promised to connect the world, have become tools for manipulation, spreading disinformation and amplifying division. These technologies are not neutral; they reflect the priorities of those who create and control them. And those priorities are clear: profit, power, and the preservation of the status quo.

Consider the role of artificial intelligence in this dystopian future. AI has the potential to revolutionize every aspect of society, from healthcare to education to governance. But in the hands of the billionaire class, it has become a tool for enforcing compliance. AI algorithms determine who gets a loan, who gets a job, who gets access to vital services. These decisions are made not with transparency or accountability but with the cold logic of profit maximization. The result is a society where inequality is baked into the code, where the powerful use technology to entrench their dominance and eliminate dissent.

The same is true of blockchain technology, which was originally envisioned as a tool for decentralization and democratization. In the world of technofeudalism, blockchain is co-opted to serve the interests of the elite. Decentralized currencies become speculative assets, enriching a small minority while leaving the majority to navigate a volatile and opaque financial system. Smart contracts, which could have been used to empower communities, are instead used to enforce exploitative agreements with unyielding precision. The promise of these technologies has been twisted into a tool for consolidation, a means of further concentrating wealth and power.

This vision of technofeudalism is not just a threat to economic justice; it is a threat to the very fabric of society. It undermines the principles of democracy, replacing collective decision-making with the whims of a wealthy few. It erodes the concept of citizenship, reducing people to consumers and data points. It strips away the dignity of work, turning labor into a commodity to be bought and sold at the lowest possible price. And it does all this while cloaking itself in the language of innovation and progress.

The billionaires who champion this vision do not see themselves as villains. They see themselves as visionaries, as the architects of a new world order. They believe that their wealth and power are proof of their superiority, their right to dictate the future. They see democracy as an obstacle, equality as a fantasy, and humanity as a resource to be exploited. This is not just arrogance; it is a fundamental rejection of the values that underpin a just and equitable society.

The question, then, is what we do in the face of this vision. Do we accept it as inevitable, as the natural evolution of capitalism? Or do we resist it, reject it, and fight for a different future? The answer lies in recognizing the power of collective action, in reclaiming technology as a tool for liberation rather than control. It lies in demanding accountability from the billionaire class, in exposing their lies and challenging their narratives. And it lies in building alternatives, in creating systems that prioritize people over profit, democracy over domination, and dignity over despair.

The road ahead will not be easy. The forces arrayed against us are powerful, and the vision of technofeudalism is seductive in its simplicity. But we must remember that the systems that sustain this vision are not immutable; they are constructed, and what is constructed can be dismantled. We have the tools, the knowledge, and the collective power to build a different future. It is up to us to decide whether we will use them.

The billionaires may believe that they are untouchable, that their vision of technofeudalism is inevitable. But history has shown us that no system, no matter how entrenched, is beyond challenge. The waters are rising, and the rock on which they stand is not as solid as it seems. The question is not whether we can resist, but whether we will choose to. The future is ours to shape, if only we have the courage to claim it.

The billionaires' vision of technofeudalism is not just an economic construct; it is a calculated effort to reshape humanity itself. The systems they champion are designed to control not only the material aspects of our lives but the psychological, social, and spiritual dimensions as well. At the heart of their dystopian ambition lies an insidious truth: their power relies on the systematic dehumanization of everyone outside their elite circle. They do not simply hoard wealth; they hoard agency, ensuring that the masses remain trapped in cycles of dependence and compliance. This is not the natural evolution of technology or society; it is a deliberate strategy to cement their dominance, one algorithm, one law, one decision at a time.

Part of what makes this vision so dangerous is its seductive appeal. The rhetoric of innovation, progress, and disruption masks the true purpose of their actions. They frame their projects as solutions to global problems, as advancements that will improve the quality of life for all. But when we peel back the layers of marketing and media hype, we see the reality: their innovations serve primarily to reinforce their own power. Consider the rise of the so-called "smart city," a concept lauded as the future of urban living. On the surface, it promises efficiency, sustainability, and convenience. In practice, it becomes a laboratory for surveillance, a space where every movement, every transaction, every interaction is monitored, recorded, and monetized.

84

These smart cities are not designed for the people who live in them; they are designed for the corporations that profit from them. The data collected from residents is not used to empower communities but to sell products, predict behavior, and optimize control. Public spaces are privatized, infrastructure is tailored to the needs of the wealthy, and the poor are pushed further into the margins. The same pattern emerges in other industries championed by the billionaire class. Renewable energy, for example, could democratize access to power, allowing communities to generate and share their own electricity.

Instead, it is being monopolized by corporations that prioritize profit over accessibility, turning a potential tool for liberation into yet another mechanism of control. This pattern is repeated across every sector where technology intersects with basic human needs. Healthcare becomes a luxury market, where life-saving treatments are priced for profit rather than necessity. Education is commodified, with elite schools and personalized learning tools reserved for those who can afford them. Even the dream of space exploration, once a symbol of collective human achievement, is now reduced to a billionaire's vanity project, an escape hatch for the few rather than a frontier for all.

The psychological impact of living under such a system is profound. It erodes not only material security but also the sense of agency and solidarity that gives life meaning. In this techno-feudal society, despair is cultivated as a tool of control. The narratives of self-reliance and individual failure are amplified, convincing people that their struggles are personal shortcomings rather than systemic injustices. Meanwhile, the billionaire class exploits these insecurities, offering just enough convenience and distraction to keep the masses docile. They manipulate public perception, using media they own and fund to manufacture consent and normalize inequality. In their vision, a society of isolated individuals is easier to control than a united community.

This control extends into the spiritual and emotional realms. The billionaire class seeks to reshape our very understanding of fulfillment, replacing the idea of collective well-being with the pursuit of consumer satisfaction. They bombard us with images of what we should desire, luxury, exclusivity, and unattainable wealth, while ensuring that these aspirations remain out of reach for most. This endless cycle of wanting and failing is not an accident; it is a carefully crafted system designed to keep us striving for goals that benefit them, not us.

But beneath the polished facade of innovation lies a far more insidious truth: the billionaires' vision is fundamentally unsustainable. Their unchecked greed undermines the very systems they rely on. The environmental devastation they perpetuate threatens the habitability of the planet itself. Climate change, resource depletion, and mass extinction are not distant concerns but immediate crises exacerbated by their insatiable pursuit of profit. Their solutions, geoengineering, luxury survival bunkers, and interplanetary colonization, are nothing more than escapes for the elite, leaving the rest of humanity to bear the brunt of their destruction.

This is not progress. It is regression, a return to a feudal order where power is concentrated in the hands of a few and the majority are left to toil in servitude. The difference is that today's lords are not bound by geography or tradition. Their empires are global, their influence unrestrained by national borders or democratic accountability. They are building a world where technology reinforces their power, where dissent is crushed by algorithms, and where the future is dictated by the whims of the wealthy.

Yet, the cracks in this vision are already visible. The billionaire class may believe they are invincible, but their power is far from absolute. Their systems are built on fragile foundations, reliant on the compliance of the masses and the stability of the planet they exploit. History has shown that no regime, no matter how entrenched, is beyond challenge. The same tools they use to dominate, technology, communication, and networks, can be turned against them.

The path to opposition begins with reclaiming these tools and reimagining their potential. Technology can serve as a force for democratization rather than control. Decentralized platforms, open-source software, and community-driven innovations offer glimpses of a different future, one where power is distributed rather than hoarded. These initiatives are not just technical solutions; they are acts of defiance, a rejection of the billionaire class's monopoly on innovation.

Education must play a central role in this opposition. We must teach people, especially the next generation, to see through the myths propagated by the billionaire class. Stories of collective struggle and grassroots victories must replace the sanitized narratives of entrepreneurial genius. Critical thinking, civic engagement, and a deep understanding of history are essential tools for dismantling the structures of technofeudalism. These are not just skills; they are weapons in the fight for a just and equitable future.

Economic opposition is equally important. The billionaire class thrives on systems that prioritize profit over people, but those systems are vulnerable. Labor strikes, consumer boycotts, and the creation of cooperative economies challenge their dominance. Policy changes, such as progressive taxation, universal basic income, and public ownership of essential services, can redistribute power and resources. These measures are not merely reforms; they are steps toward dismantling the economic foundations of billionaire control.

The most powerful form of opposition, however, is solidarity. The billionaire class wants us divided, isolated, and disempowered. But history proves that collective action is the greatest force for change. When communities come together, they can challenge even the most entrenched systems. From the labor movements of the 19th century to the civil rights struggles of the 20th, progress has always been driven by those who refuse to accept the status quo. The future will be no different.

Challenge yourself and others to imagine a world free from the grip of technofeudalism. This is not just an exercise in hope; it is a necessary step toward creating the future we deserve. The systems that oppress us are not immutable; they are constructed, and what is constructed can be dismantled. The billionaires may believe they have secured their place at the top, but their vision is not inevitable. It is up to us to expose their lies, reject their control, and build a world where humanity, not profit, is the ultimate measure of progress. The fight will not be easy, but it is one worth waging, for ourselves, for future generations, and for the planet we call home.

*The term "technofeudalism" was popularized by Yanis Varoufakis in *Technofeudalism: What Killed Capitalism* (2023), though Michel Luc Bellemare introduced a similar concept, "techno-capitalist-feudalism," in 2020.

What You Can Do: Boycott, Who & Why

The most prominent techno-feudalists, figures like Elon Musk, Jeff Bezos, Mark Zuckerberg, Larry Page, Marc Andreessen, and Peter Thiel, represent the apex of a system that prioritizes profit and control over humanity and democracy. Their empires, built on the exploitation of labor, data, and resources, have redefined the boundaries of power, creating a digital aristocracy that dictates how we work, communicate, and live. Each of these figures champions a vision of the future where they reign as untouchable overlords, consolidating wealth and influence at the expense of the many.

Elon Musk, with ventures like Tesla and SpaceX, positions himself as a savior of humanity while exploiting workers and opposing unionization. Jeff Bezos built Amazon into a global behemoth by normalizing worker surveillance and driving small businesses into extinction. Mark Zuckerberg's Meta (formerly Facebook) monetizes division and disinformation while amassing unprecedented control over global communication. Larry Page and Google have turned information into a commodity, tracking and selling every detail of our digital lives. Peter Thiel actively funds anti-democratic ideologies, pushing for a world of techno-feudal city-states where billionaires hold unchecked power and are already running the administration out in the open, the politicians are their prostitute puppets. "Donate" a few million and benefit a few billion, not a bad deal.

Boycotting their products and platforms is an act of defiance. Unplugging from Amazon, Facebook, Instagram, and other tools of exploitation reclaims our autonomy and denies them the data and dollars they use to tighten their grip. Supporting local businesses, open-source platforms, and ethical alternatives disrupts their dominance. It sends a clear message: we will not fund our own oppression. Change begins when we refuse to comply with systems designed to exploit us and instead build new ones that prioritize community, fairness, and sustainability.

The teenager had always known the town was small, but now it felt suffocating. The roads seemed narrower, the houses closer together, and the air heavier. There was a sense that something unseen pressed down on everything, draining the life from the place. It wasn't until recently that they began to understand the source of that weight. The billionaire, whose name everyone whispered but no one spoke aloud, was more than a man in their eyes now. He was a shadow, a presence, an entity whose wealth and influence stretched far beyond the walls of his distant mansion. The billionaire is not so much as a man but as an unholy force, a specter that hovered over the town, shaping its every corner.

The family's modest home, once a refuge, now felt like a cage. The teenager looked out the window and saw the subtle signs of the billionaire's reach. The factory, where their parent had worked for decades, stood silent and abandoned, its windows shattered and its gates rusted shut. Around it, the grass grew wild, reclaiming the space in a way that felt both defiant and mournful. But the factory's closure had left a scar that went deeper than the physical decay. It had marked the town itself, replacing hope with resignation and community with survival.

The teenager's vision of the billionaire shifted with every passing day. They no longer thought of him as a person. He had become a myth, a symbol of something much larger and darker. The billionaire blurred the line between man and monster, portraying the billionaire as a figure whose power was so vast it seemed unnatural. His wealth wasn't just a number; it was an extension of himself, an endless reach that touched every life in the town. The teenager imagined him as a grotesque being, his form twisted by greed, his face a mask of charm hiding something ancient and cruel.

The changes in the town were subtle at first, almost easy to miss. Cameras appeared on street corners, their lenses gleaming like watchful eyes. No one knew who had installed them, but everyone assumed they were linked to the billionaire. Then came the automated systems: the self-checkout machines at the grocery store, the kiosks at the post office, the online portals for everything from utility payments to job applications. Each new system promised convenience, but the teenager saw them for what they were, another way to strip people of their agency, to replace human connection with cold efficiency. The machines weren't just tools; they were symbols of control, reminders that the billionaire's influence extended even into their daily routines.

Life took on a dreamlike quality, weaving horror and reality together until they were inseparable. The teenager walked the streets of the town and felt as though they were being watched, not just by the cameras but by something else, something intangible. They noticed how people moved more quietly, spoke in hushed tones, and avoided eye contact. It was as if the billionaire's presence had seeped into the very fabric of the town, turning it into a place of shadows and silence. The teenager couldn't shake the feeling that they were being swallowed by something too vast to fight.

Their anger simmered beneath the surface, fueled by a growing sense of injustice. One night, they confronted their parents at the dinner table, their voice shaking with frustration. "Why do we let this happen?" they asked, their eyes darting between their mother and father. "Why do we let him take everything from us?" Their parents exchanged weary glances, their faces etched with lines of worry and fatigue. "Because we don't have a choice," their mother said softly. "You can't fight someone like him. He's too big. Too powerful."

The teenager slammed their fist on the table, the sound echoing through the small kitchen. "That's what he wants you to think! That's how he wins! By making us believe we're powerless!" Their father sighed and looked away, his shoulders slumping as though under an invisible weight. "It's not about what we believe," he said, his voice heavy. "It's about what's real. And what's real is that people who stand up to him don't win. They just disappear."

The teenager's frustration boiled into fury. They couldn't understand how their parents accepted this, how they lived knowing their lives were controlled by someone who didn't even know their names. But as days passed, their anger transformed into something else, a fire, a determination to see the billionaire for what he truly was and find a way to stop him against all odds. The turning point came one night as the teenager walked home alone. The air was thick with humidity, the sky a dark, oppressive gray. As they passed the abandoned factory, a chill ran down their spine. The building loomed in the darkness, its broken windows like hollow eyes staring at the town. They paused, breath catching as a strange sensation washed over them. It was as if the factory itself was alive, its walls pulsing with an energy they couldn't explain.

The teenager's footsteps echoed against the pavement, each step growing louder in the night's stillness. The shadows around them seemed to move, twisting as if alive. And then, out of the corner of their eye, they saw him. The billionaire. He stood near the factory gates, his figure obscured by darkness. But even in the shadows, his presence was undeniable. He exuded a strange, almost magnetic energy, a mix of menace and allure that left the teenager frozen. The encounter was dreamlike, surreal, terrifying. The billionaire stepped closer, his features becoming clearer in the dim light. He was dressed impeccably, his suit sharp, his shoes gleaming. But something was wrong, something unnatural. His eyes seemed too bright, his smile too perfect, his movements too smooth. He wasn't just a man; he was a presence, a force that defied explanation. The teenager felt a surge of fear and anger, their mind racing. Was this what power looked like? Was this the man who had taken so much from their family, their town, their future?

The swirling smoke obscured the factory's silhouette, thick and suffocating, but within it, faint shapes flickered, small children, barely visible. Why was smoke rising from a factory long shut down? The air reeked of more than decay. It felt as though the billionaire was burning something else, he stolen futures of these children, their potential turned to ash to sustain his insatiable hunger for wealth and domination. This was more than greed, more than corruption. It was monstrous. The factory had been an illusion of progress once, but now it stood as an altar to destruction. The teenager knew this was a battle of good versus evil.

From within the smoke, a figure emerged, smooth and untouchable. The billionaire stepped forward, his voice calm yet venomous. "You're one of the curious ones," he said, almost amused. "That's good. Curiosity is useful. But be careful. It can also be dangerous." The teenager's breath hitched. They wanted to demand answers, but their voice caught in their throat. The billionaire's smile widened, too perfect, too practiced. "You're wondering why I'm here," he continued. "The truth is, I'm always here. Everywhere. Watching. Listening. Guiding. You can't escape me. No one can."

Fear clawed at the teenager, but anger burned brighter. They clenched their fists and took a step forward. "You're not invincible," they said, voice trembling but firm. "You think you control everything, but you don't. People won't let you." The billionaire's eyes narrowed, his mask faltering for a moment before he laughed, low and menacing. "We'll see about that," he said. "We'll see."

The encounter left the teenager shaken but resolute. They had seen beyond wealth and corruption, they had seen evil itself. The billionaire wasn't just a man. He was something darker, something that needed to be confronted. The truth could not stay buried. The stolen futures, the smoke, the factory, none of it could be unseen. The teenager steadied their breath. They weren't just afraid anymore. They were ready.

WE
SEE
YOU

The teenager couldn't sleep after that night. Their encounter with the billionaire replayed in their mind like a haunting melody, each word and movement etched into their memory. The idea of him being "always here" lingered like a poison, infecting their thoughts. The teenager realized that the billionaire's power wasn't just in his wealth or his influence, it was in the fear he instilled, the way he made people believe he was untouchable. But even in the depths of their unease, a new thought began to take shape: what if he wasn't?

The next morning, the teenager woke up with a sense of purpose. They weren't sure what they would do, but they knew they couldn't stay silent. They began by visiting the library, a quiet building tucked away at the edge of town. It was one of the few places that hadn't yet been touched by the billionaire's influence, at least, not overtly. The shelves smelled of old paper and dust, and the librarian, an elderly woman with sharp eyes, gave them a curious look as they entered.

"What are you looking for?" she asked, her voice soft but firm.

"Information," the teenager replied. "About him. The billionaire."

The librarian's expression darkened, and she glanced around nervously before leaning in. "Careful who you talk to about that," she whispered. "He's got ears everywhere." But despite her warning, she led the teenager to a section of old newspapers and pointed to a stack in the corner. "Start there," she said. "But don't tell anyone I helped you."

For hours, the teenager pored over the newspapers, their hands smudged with ink as they flipped through page after page. Most of the articles were vague, praising the billionaire's "investments" in the town or celebrating his "philanthropy." But every so often, they found a hint of something darker: a factory worker who had mysteriously disappeared after organizing a union, a local journalist who had abruptly left town after publishing a critical piece, a small business that had shut down under suspicious circumstances. The teenager pieced together a picture of a man who wielded power not just through wealth, but through intimidation and silence.

As the days turned into weeks, the teenager began to notice patterns. The billionaire's empire wasn't built on generosity or goodwill, it was built on fear, exploitation, and control. They started to see how the town's systems were designed to benefit him, from the overpriced utilities to the unregulated rents. Even the cameras on the street corners seemed to serve no purpose other than to remind everyone who was in charge.

But the more the teenager learned, the more they began to see cracks in the façade. For all his power, the billionaire was still human, or at least, he operated within human systems. And systems could be disrupted.

The teenager's first act of defiance was small but symbolic. They took a can of spray paint and, under the cover of darkness, scrawled the words "WE SEE YOU" across the side of one of the billionaire's automated kiosks. It wasn't much, but it was a start. The next morning, they walked past the kiosk on their way to school and felt a surge of pride when they saw people stopping to look at the message. A few even nodded in approval before hurrying on their way.

Encouraged by the reaction, the teenager decided to take things further. They began talking to their classmates, carefully choosing those they thought might share their frustration. At first, the conversations were hesitant, filled with nervous glances and whispered words. But as more people joined in, the group grew bolder. They shared stories of how the billionaire's influence had affected their families: a parent who had lost their job, a sibling forced to move away for work, a friend who couldn't afford to stay in town.

It wasn't long before the group started organizing. They called themselves "The Shadows," a nod to the way they operated under the radar, avoiding the billionaire's watchful eyes. They met in secret, usually at the library or in abandoned buildings, and began brainstorming ways to challenge the systems that kept the town under his control. Their goal wasn't just to disrupt, they wanted to inspire others to see that opposition was possible.

One night, The Shadows staged their first coordinated action. They hacked into the town's public announcement system, a network of speakers that had been installed under the guise of emergency preparedness but mostly played advertisements for the billionaire's businesses. Instead of the usual messages, the speakers crackled to life with a recording of a distorted voice:

"To the people of this town: You are not powerless. He wants you to believe that you are, but you're not. Together, we can fight back. Together, we can take back what's ours. The Shadows are with you."

The message played on a loop for nearly an hour before the system was shut down. By then, word had already spread. The town buzzed with whispers about the mysterious message, and for the first time in years, there was a sense of hope in the air.

The billionaire's response was swift and brutal. The next day, a team of workers arrived to repair the announcement system, and the cameras on the street corners were upgraded. New posters appeared around town, warning against "illegal activities" and urging residents to report any suspicious behavior. But The Shadows weren't deterred. If anything, the billionaire's reaction only confirmed that their efforts were having an impact.

The teenager, now one of the group's unofficial leaders, felt a mix of fear and exhilaration. They knew the risks were growing, but so was their determination. They started spending more time at the library, combing through old books on activism and opposition. They learned about movements that had fought against impossible odds and found inspiration in stories of ordinary people who had stood up to power.

The teenager also began to notice something unexpected: the cracks in the billionaire's control weren't just systemic, they were personal. Despite his wealth and influence, he seemed desperate to maintain an image of invincibility. The posters, the cameras, the automated systems, they weren't just tools of control; they were signs of insecurity, a way to hide the fact that his power wasn't as absolute as he wanted people to believe.

As The Shadows continued their actions, the town began to change. People started speaking out, sharing their stories and demanding answers. A group of former factory workers organized a protest outside the gates of the abandoned building, holding signs that read "WE BUILT THIS TOWN" and "WE DESERVE BETTER." Local artists painted murals depicting scenes of community and resilience, transforming the gray walls of the town into vibrant symbols of defiance.

The teenager felt a sense of pride every time they walked through the streets. The town that had once felt suffocating now felt alive with possibility. But they also knew that the fight was far from over. The billionaire wasn't going to give up his control without a fight, and The Shadows would need to be ready for whatever came next.

One evening, as the teenager sat by their bedroom window, they saw a flicker of movement outside. At first, they thought it was their imagination. But then they noticed a figure standing under the streetlight, staring up at their house. It was the billionaire.

He was dressed as impeccably as ever, his suit unwrinkled and his shoes gleaming. But there was something different about him now. His face, usually a mask of confidence, looked strained, almost desperate. He raised a hand and pointed directly at the teenager's window, his eyes gleaming in the dim light.

The teenager felt a chill run down their spine but refused to look away. They held his gaze, their heart pounding in their chest. The billionaire's expression shifted, his lips curling into a thin, humorless smile. And then, without a word, he turned and walked away, disappearing into the shadows.

The teenager sat frozen for a moment, their mind racing. The encounter had shaken them, but it also filled them with a renewed sense of purpose. The billionaire might have been watching, but so were they. And they weren't going to stop.

The battle for the town was just beginning.

The Unnaturalness of Greed

The teenager's evolving perception of the billionaire reveals a deeper truth about the nature of greed: it is not just a destructive force but an unnatural one. Greed, especially in its modern, industrialized form, goes beyond simple human frailty. It becomes an ideology, a system designed to extract more than it gives and to take without regard for what is left behind. The teenager's town, once alive with the rhythms of community and work, now feels like a corpse animated by machines and controlled by invisible hands. This transformation, while seemingly inevitable, is anything but natural. It is the product of a carefully constructed framework of exploitation that serves a singular purpose: the consolidation of wealth and power.

The billionaire is no longer merely a man in the teenager's mind but a grotesque emblem of this system, unchecked capitalism, a living metaphor for the ways greed twists and contorts reality. His very presence is a distortion, a reminder that his wealth does not flow from some boundless source but from the very lifeblood of others. His power is not earned; it is siphoned. The teenager begins to see the billionaire's acts of "philanthropy" not as gestures of goodwill but as grotesque parodies of generosity. Every new camera, every automated system, every gleaming kiosk is presented as a gift to the town, a promise of efficiency and progress. Yet these so-called gifts do not enrich lives; they diminish them, trading humanity for convenience and connection for control. And when they take the government "gifts" for themselves it is the old adage, socialism for me but not for thee, never mind that libraries, school, police, and fire departments are all socialism for we.

This is the essence of technofeudalism, a system where wealth operates not as a tool for betterment but as a mechanism of domination. The billionaire's influence extends into every corner of the teenager's world, from the abandoned factory to the quiet resignation etched into their parents' faces. Technofeudalism replaces community with surveillance, agency with automation, and hope with resignation. It is not merely inhuman but anti-human, an affront to the very essence of living with dignity and freedom.

102

The teenager begins to understand that this system is not invincible. It is built on the belief that people are powerless to resist, that their fears will outweigh their hopes. The billionaire thrives not because he is untouchable but because he has convinced others of his untouchability. Yet this realization, while empowering, also fills the teenager with a sense of dread. To see the system for what it is means acknowledging its profound wrongness, a wrongness so vast and insidious that it feels almost otherworldly.

The teenager's anger crystallizes into a quiet, burning resolve. The billionaire is no longer just a man to them; he is an idea, a force that must be confronted. And while they do not yet know how to fight back, they understand that to do nothing is to accept defeat. This realization marks a turning point, not just for the teenager but for the narrative itself. The billionaire's greed, stripped of its façade, reveals its true nature: a parasitic force that feeds on fear and thrives on submission. The question now is whether that force can be dismantled, and whether the people it oppresses can reclaim what has been stolen from them.

Let's conclude by referring back to the image of the monstrous otter offering a shimmering, toxic fish to starving otters encapsulates the grotesque nature of billionaire vision or "gifts." What appears to be an act of generosity is, upon closer inspection, a calculated gesture of control. The giver's elongated, unnatural form and cold, predatory smile reveal its true intent: dominance and dependency. The starving otters, too desperate to question the gift, are ensnared by the giver's shadow, much like the teenager's realization that the billionaire's systems, his cameras, kiosks, and automation, are not symbols of progress but chains of control, turning greed into an unnatural, all-consuming force.

Chapter 4
How Billionaires Rewrite History

Let's talk about the emperor with no clothes, shall we? Except in this version, he's not just prancing around naked, he's hoarding food, evicting families, and building glass towers to look down on the rest of us while insisting it's all perfectly rational. That's what billionaires have done to our sense of reality. They've created an upside-down world where egg prices doubling overnight and entire cities becoming unlivable are shrugged off as the "natural order." We're told it's all just supply and demand, or a "market correction," as if these absurdities are cosmic inevitabilities instead of engineered disasters. And here's the kicker: they don't just want us to tolerate this madness, they want us to believe it's sane.

This isn't some unfortunate byproduct of a flawed system. No, this is the system. Billionaires control the narrative because they control the storytellers: the media outlets, the school curriculums, the think tanks. They pump out propaganda faster than they pump oil out of the ground, all to convince us that their greed-fueled chaos is progress. Meanwhile, they erase the stories that could inspire us to fight back, stories of labor revolts, union victories, and ordinary people demanding something better. What's left is a curated history that glorifies them as the saviors of a world they're actively destroying.

And let's not ignore how they turn us against each other to keep their empires intact. Billionaire-funded media loves a scapegoat, whether it's immigrants, activists, or entire communities labeled as "undeserving." They're masters of "othering," because a divided society is an obedient one. Mass deportation centers, surveillance cameras on every corner, and endless rhetoric about "law and order," sound familiar? It should. We've seen this playbook before, and it didn't end well the first time around. But here's the ugly truth: these aren't just echoes of history; they're active blueprints for the dystopia they're building.

What's their endgame? Simple. They want a world where their greed isn't just accepted, it's worshipped. They're not building a future for humanity; they're building one for themselves. A gated paradise where democracy is a quaint relic and collective action is a bad memory. They want us atomized, distracted, and docile, too busy scrambling for scraps to realize the whole table is rigged.

And here's the part they don't want you to think about: this level of greed isn't natural. It's not human. Call it a virus of the soul, call it demonic possession, call it whatever you want, but tell me, honestly, does it look like humanity to you? These billionaires, with their unrelenting hunger for wealth and power, have turned themselves into something else entirely. They're not just hoarders, they're predators, and they'll strip this planet bare if we let them.

So, ask yourself: what's our capacity for opposition? Because that's what they're really testing. They're daring us to see through their illusions, to call out their lies, to fight back against their empire of greed. And if we don't? Well, the emperor might not need clothes, but we're the ones who'll end up exposed.

Let us begin with a foundational truth: the stories we tell ourselves shape the world we live in. Narratives are not just tales of the past or speculations about the future, they are frameworks that define what we believe to be possible, acceptable, and even inevitable. Billionaires, wielding immense power over media, education, and public discourse, understand this better than anyone. They have taken control of our collective narrative, reshaping it into something that benefits them while erasing the inconvenient truths of the past.

Their mastery lies in convincing the public that the chaos they create, whether skyrocketing egg prices, unaffordable housing, or the erosion of workers' rights, is not only inevitable but natural. This is what is called "sane-washing," a calculated reframing of absurdities to make them appear rational. By presenting themselves as the arbiters of reason, they deflect accountability for the very crises they orchestrate.

Consider the economic realities we face today. Housing prices have soared to astronomical levels while wages stagnate, and we are told this is simply the result of "market forces." These abstract concepts, "supply and demand," "inflationary pressures," and "economic cycles," are trotted out to pacify public outrage, implying that no one is to blame and nothing can be done. The billionaires, the landlords, developers, and profiteers, are conspicuously absent from this narrative. The truth, of course, is that these economic crises are not natural disasters; they are the deliberate result of policies and practices that prioritize profit over people. Yet this truth is obscured by a carefully crafted narrative that shifts focus away from systemic exploitation and onto individual responsibility or vague, uncontrollable forces.

This narrative is no accident. It is crafted and disseminated through every channel billionaires control, from media conglomerates to educational institutions. Mainstream media, owned and influenced by the wealthiest among us, reframes systemic issues as individual failings or unavoidable circumstances. Reports on homelessness, for example, often emphasize personal choices, addiction, or mental health struggles while glossing over the fact that billionaires and corporate landlords have turned housing into a commodity rather than a basic human right.

Similarly, stories about inflation rarely delve into corporate greed or price-gouging, focusing instead on "labor shortages" or "consumer demand." In this way, the media becomes a tool for shaping public perception, deflecting blame from the powerful and reinforcing the status quo.

Schools, too, play a critical role in this narrative manipulation. Our history books glorify industry titans and their so-called "innovations" while conveniently leaving out the stories of labor movements, strikes, and collective opposition. We learn about Rockefeller's philanthropy but not the brutal conditions in his refineries. We hear about Carnegie's libraries but not the Pinkertons he hired to crush unions. By erasing these inconvenient truths, billionaires ensure that future generations are taught to admire wealth rather than question it. The result is a populace primed to accept the unacceptable, too confused or demoralized to challenge the systems that oppress them.

Sane-washing also serves a more sinister purpose: it conditions us to accept billionaire control as the natural order. If the problems we face are inevitable, then so too is their dominance. The emperor with no clothes becomes the emperor we must revere, even as we feel the chill of his power stripping us bare. This rewriting of reality is not passive; it is an active and deliberate act of control. Billionaires are not content to hoard wealth and resources, they must also hoard truth, twisting it to suit their ends. This manipulation is so pervasive and insidious that it warps our very sense of reality, making us question whether we are wrong to see the emperor's nakedness while everyone else applauds his imaginary robes.

The absurdities we are told to rationalize have reached staggering proportions. Imagine, for instance, being told that the housing crisis, a crisis manufactured by speculative investors and corporate landlords, is the fault of environmental regulations or zoning laws. This is the equivalent of blaming the trees for the forest fire while the arsonist stands off to the side, matches still in hand. Or consider the narrative around inflation, where we are told to tighten our belts and accept higher prices as inevitable while CEOs boast record profits to their shareholders. These aren't merely distortions of the truth; they are outright inversions, designed to make us question our own understanding of fairness and justice.

The power of these narratives lies in their ability to shift the burden of responsibility. Instead of asking why billionaires are allowed to extract obscene wealth from housing, healthcare, and education, we are asked why we didn't save more money or make better choices. Instead of questioning why essential workers are underpaid and undervalued, we are told that they lack the skills or ambition to thrive in a "competitive market." These narratives are not just false, they are cruel, gaslighting an entire population into blaming themselves for problems that were engineered by the very people who profit from them.

This rewriting of reality also serves to insulate billionaires from accountability. By framing systemic issues as natural phenomena, they position themselves as neutral players, or worse, benevolent saviors. They present their philanthropy as proof of their moral character while conveniently ignoring that their wealth was built on exploitation. The billionaire who donates to education reform after lobbying against higher corporate taxes, the tech mogul who pledges to fight climate change while funding fossil fuel expansion, these are not acts of generosity but carefully calculated maneuvers to maintain power and deflect criticism.

The ultimate goal of sane-washing is not merely to obscure responsibility but to normalize inequality. It seeks to create a world where billionaires are not only accepted but revered, where their greed is seen as ambition, their excess as success, and their dominance as destiny. In this world, the absurd becomes routine: families forced to choose between food and medicine, students saddled with debt for the crime of seeking an education, workers clocking in at jobs that barely keep them alive. And yet, we are told this is the best we can hope for, that to ask for more would be unreasonable, even dangerous.

But let us be clear: there is nothing natural about this order. It is not the inevitable outcome of human progress or the logical conclusion of market forces. It is a construct, designed and maintained by those who benefit most from it. Billionaires are not passive beneficiaries of this system; they are its architects and enforcers. They have shaped the rules to serve their interests, and they have shaped the stories we tell ourselves to make those rules seem fair.

This is why the battle for truth is so critical. To challenge the power of billionaires, we must first challenge the narratives they have imposed on us. We must unearth the stories they have buried, stories of workers demanding justice, communities resisting exploitation, and ordinary people daring to dream of a better world. We must expose the emperor for what he is, standing naked and unashamed, while the rest of us suffer under the weight of his illusions.

The task is daunting, but it is not impossible. The power of stories cuts both ways. Just as billionaires have used them to justify their greed, we can use them to reclaim our humanity. By telling the truth about their power and its consequences, we can begin to dismantle the systems that sustain it. The emperor may have convinced us that his clothes are real, but deep down, we know the truth. It is time to say it out loud.

Write or draw a piece of history you know to be true below:

The next few weeks were a whirlwind of activity for The Shadows. What had started as a small group of disaffected teenagers and quietly frustrated residents was now growing into something larger, a movement. The teenager marveled at how quickly their acts of defiance had inspired others to step forward. Quiet grumblings in coffee shops turned into late-night meetings, hushed conversations between neighbors evolved into small gatherings, and those gatherings gave way to plans for action. The sense of hopeless resignation that had long hung over the town began to lift, replaced by a cautious but undeniable sense of hope.

The group's next act was more ambitious. They decided to target one of the billionaire's most visible symbols of control: the sprawling mall on the edge of town. It had once been a bustling community space, full of local shops and small businesses. But over the years, as rents skyrocketed, the independent businesses had been forced out, replaced by sleek corporate chains owned or funded by the billionaire. Even the mall itself bore his name in towering letters above its entrance.

The plan was simple but symbolic. The Shadows intended to project a message onto the mall's facade, one that could not be ignored. They had recruited a local tech-savvy member who rigged a projector to display an enormous image on the building. On a dark, overcast night, as the mall's parking lot sat nearly empty, the words blazed across the front: "HIS GREED, OUR RUIN." The image was accompanied by silhouettes of people standing together, their fists raised in defiance.

The effect was immediate. Cars stopped in the street as drivers gawked at the display. Passersby gathered, some taking pictures, others murmuring in agreement. The projection stayed up for nearly fifteen minutes before mall security arrived, but by then, it had already been shared widely on social media. The hashtag #HisGreedOurRuin began trending in the region, drawing attention far beyond the confines of the town.

The billionaire's response was swift and calculated. Within days, the mall had installed brighter floodlights and more cameras. The local news, which was heavily influenced by his media empire, ran a segment decrying the act as "vandalism" and warning against the rise of "anti-progress extremists." But for The Shadows, the success of their message was undeniable. It was clear now: people were paying attention.

As The Shadows grew, so did the teenager's awareness of the billionaire's vulnerabilities. It wasn't just the systems of control that revealed cracks but the man himself. The teenager started to notice patterns in his appearances, almost as if he were trying to maintain a looming presence but overextending in the process.

At ribbon-cutting ceremonies for new developments, his smile seemed forced, his posture rigid. At town hall meetings, he appeared briefly, delivering rehearsed platitudes before disappearing behind closed doors. Rumors began to swirl about his temper, about his health, about the strained relationships within his inner circle. These were whispers carried on the wind, but to the teenager, they hinted at something more profound, a man desperate to keep the illusion of invincibility intact.

The group began to capitalize on this growing awareness. They used social media to share stories that had been suppressed for years: accounts of workers mistreated in the billionaire's factories, local businesses shuttered by his monopolistic practices, families displaced by his insatiable appetite for development. Each post was accompanied by a simple message: "We see you."

People started to come forward with their own stories. An older woman shared how her father had been fired from the factory after attempting to unionize. A young couple posted about their eviction from a building purchased and immediately renovated by one of the billionaire's shell companies. Each story added weight to the movement, painting a fuller picture of the harm he had caused.

For all their successes, The Shadows knew they were playing a dangerous game. The billionaire was not a man to tolerate dissent. The new posters warning against "illegal activities" had multiplied, plastered across walls and telephone poles in every neighborhood. Anonymous tip lines were established, offering

114

rewards for information leading to the identification of the individuals behind the growing unrest.

The teenager noticed an increase in the presence of security forces around town, not police, but private contractors dressed in dark uniforms, their faces obscured by sunglasses and caps. Their vans, unmarked but conspicuous, began patrolling the streets at irregular intervals. It was clear that the billionaire's response was escalating, and The Shadows began to feel the pressure.

One night, as they met in the library's basement, a sense of unease hung heavy in the air. The librarian, their reluctant ally, warned them of increased surveillance. "Be careful," she said, her voice low. "He's watching more closely than ever." Despite her caution, the group pressed on, emboldened by the growing number of supporters joining their cause.

But the billionaire's reach extended further than they could have anticipated. One member of The Shadows, a young man named Marcus, failed to show up at a planned meeting. His absence stretched into days, and no one could reach him. When the teenager finally went to his house, they found his family shaken and tight-lipped. "It's better if you don't ask," his mother said, her voice trembling. The teenager left with a sinking feeling, realizing that Marcus's disappearance was a message, a warning.
The pressure mounted, and with it came the nightmares. The teenager began to dream of the billionaire as something monstrous, his human form giving way to shadow and flame. In one recurring vision, they stood in the abandoned factory, its walls crumbling around them. From the darkness emerged the billionaire, his body elongated and grotesque, his eyes glowing with an unnatural light. His voice, deep and resonant, filled the space: "You think you've won something, don't you? But you haven't even begun to lose."

These dreams, though terrifying, also fueled the teenager's resolve. They began to see the billionaire not as an untouchable figure but as a symbol of everything they were fighting against. His monstrous visage was a manifestation of his greed, his desire to control and consume without limit. And while the dreams left the teenager shaken, they also served as a reminder of what was at stake.

The Shadows knew they needed a decisive act to galvanize the town and make it impossible for the billionaire to ignore their demands. They decided to stage a public demonstration, something visible, something undeniable. The plan was ambitious: to project their message not just onto a building but into the very heart of the billionaire's empire.

On a cold, clear night, The Shadows gathered near the town square. Armed with a powerful projector and a generator, they aimed their message at the headquarters of one of the billionaire's companies. The building, a sleek and towering structure of glass and steel, reflected the light of their projection as the words appeared: "HIS POWER IS A LIE. OUR POWER IS REAL."

The demonstration was a success beyond their expectations. Hundreds gathered to witness it, some cheering, others simply watching in awe. For a moment, it felt as though the town itself had come alive, its people united in defiance.

The billionaire's response was immediate. News outlets decried the act as an "attack on progress," while authorities announced measures to "ensure public safety." But the teenager knew the truth: they had struck a nerve. The billionaire's empire, for all its power, was not invincible. In the weeks that followed, the town began to change. Posters warning against dissent were torn down, replaced by signs of solidarity. Local artists created murals celebrating opposition, depicting unity and hope.

The teenager felt both pride and apprehension. The fight was far from over, and the billionaire wouldn't relinquish control easily. But for the first time, they saw a glimmer of what could be, a town no longer living in fear, a community united against oppression. As they stood in the square, surrounded by friends and strangers, the spark of defiance grew into something larger. It was no longer just their fight; it was everyone's. The battle was just beginning, but for the first time, they believed they could win.

116

The billionaire's empire began to crack under the weight of opposition. Whispers of discontent spread beyond the town. Social media, once a tool for control, became a battleground for truth. Videos of the teenager's defiance went viral, inspiring others to question systems of power. Hashtags like #WeAreTheChange trended globally, connecting the town's struggle to a broader movement against greed and authoritarianism.

The billionaire's attempts to suppress the uprising only fueled the flames. The teenager, once anonymous, became a symbol of courage, their name chanted in rallies and scrawled on walls. Yet, with attention came greater risk. The billionaire's enforcers grew more aggressive, and the teenager knew they were being watched. But the tide was turning. The people were no longer passive; they were awake, angry, and ready to fight for a future free from exploitation.

LIES
LIES

Sane-Washing the Grotesque: Billionaires & "Reality"

The teenager's discoveries, though deeply personal, echo a broader truth: billionaires do not merely amass wealth and power, they shape reality itself. Their influence seeps into every corner of society, manipulating the way we understand the world and our place in it. What the teenager has uncovered in forgotten archives and whispered stories is not just the erasure of history but the construction of a new, distorted narrative, a carefully curated illusion designed to mask the grotesque truth of their rule.

This distortion begins with what is called "sane-washing," the billionaire tactic of reframing injustice, exploitation, and destruction as rational, even inevitable. Through this lens, mass deportation centers are no longer viewed as cruel and inhumane; they are branded as "security measures" necessary to preserve order. Rising costs of living, which push families into poverty while corporations rake in record profits, are reframed as "market corrections," natural adjustments in an impartial system. Even environmental destruction, the razing of forests, the poisoning of rivers, the warming of our planet, is sanitized and sold to us as "progress," a necessary cost of innovation and development.

The grotesque becomes ordinary through repetition and strategic messaging. Billionaires use their media empires, their political puppets, and their corporate spokespeople to flood the public consciousness with these narratives. They strip away the human cost and replace it with sterile, economic language: "efficiency," "growth," "security." By doing so, they paralyze opposition. How can you fight what is framed as inevitable? How can you oppose what is presented as reason itself?

The teenager's journey reveals the insidiousness of this strategy. As they uncover the stories of labor movements crushed under the billionaire's heel, they begin to see the pattern: opposition is always reframed as chaos, as an assault on the "natural order." Those who challenge power are cast as radicals, troublemakers, or threats to stability. Even the memories of their defiance are erased, leaving behind only the billionaire's version of history, a version where their greed is recast as generosity and their domination as leadership.

Sane-washing does more than obscure the truth; it rewrites it. Take, for example, the destruction of the local factory that once employed most of the town. In the teenager's school lessons, its closure was described as an unfortunate but necessary step toward modernization. The billionaire was praised for bringing "new opportunities" to the area, even as unemployment soared and families were forced to leave. The reality, that the factory's closure was driven by profit margins and a deliberate strategy to exploit cheaper labor elsewhere, was buried beneath a mountain of corporate doublespeak.

This manipulation extends to the present. The teenager sees it in the cameras that watch their every move, presented as tools of "public safety," but in reality serving to enforce compliance and stifle dissent. They see it in the automated kiosks and systems that have replaced human interaction, sold to the town as "convenience" but stripping away community and agency. They see it in the billionaire's philanthropic gestures, donations to schools, sponsorships of local events, that paint him as a benefactor while distracting from the harm he causes.

The genius of sane-washing lies in its ability to make the grotesque seem normal. The billionaire's wealth, which should be seen as an obscene hoarding of resources that could lift entire communities out of poverty, is instead celebrated as the reward for his "hard work." His domination of the town's economy, which should provoke outrage, is reframed as necessary leadership, a stabilizing force in uncertain times. And the suffering he causes, the shuttered businesses, the displaced families, the environmental degradation, is dismissed as collateral damage, an unfortunate but unavoidable side effect of progress. For the teenager, these realizations are both empowering and terrifying. The billionaire's power is not just material but psychological. His ability to control the narrative maintains his grip on the town. As long as people believe his lies, as long as they accept his version of reality, they remain paralyzed, unable to imagine an alternative.

120

But the teenager sees cracks in the facade. The stories they've uncovered, accounts of labor strikes, acts of defiance, and moments of opposition, prove the billionaire's control is not absolute. These buried stories linger like embers, waiting to be reignited.

Truth cannot be entirely erased. The otter scratching into the tree is a perfect metaphor, clawing away at history to replace it with its own mark, just as billionaires erase Black history, dismantle DEI programs, and silence Latino, Indigenous, and female contributions while benefiting from those very systems. Their hypocrisy is endless: they denounce handouts while hoarding subsidies, insist history should not be "rewritten" while actively rewriting it.

Billionaire power is sustained not just by wealth but by controlling narratives. Their history is myth, their exploitation framed as progress, their destruction rebranded as innovation. But history cannot be so easily erased. The voices of Black activists, Indigenous leaders, and labor organizers remain, waiting to be reclaimed. The billionaire may scratch away at reality, but truth resurfaces. The grotesque remains normalized only if we allow it. The billionaire's mask holds only if we refuse to look beneath it. Seeing through the lies is the first act of defiance. Speaking the truth is the second. From there, opposition grows. The otter claws at the tree, but beneath the scratches, history waits to be reclaimed.

Protesting Corporations: Have a Plan

Corporations are the financial engine that powers political corruption. By funding campaigns, lobbying, and dark money organizations, they ensure policies favor profits over people. To challenge this stranglehold, opposition must focus on exposing and disrupting the corporate-political pipeline. This aligns with the principles of TIDE (Target, Inspire, Disrupt, Empower), a framework for dismantling systemic greed and corruption. Here's how corporations can be effectively protested:

Target Their Public Image
Corporations thrive on public trust and brand loyalty. Boycotts, social media campaigns, and viral actions that expose unethical practices force them to address public outrage. Targeting their image disrupts their ability to maintain control over narratives and public perception.

Inspire Worker Opposition
Workers are the backbone of corporate power. Supporting unionization efforts, amplifying whistleblowers, and organizing workplace actions inspire opposition from within. Empowered workers can challenge exploitative practices and shift the balance of power.

Disrupt Their Revenue Streams
Corporations rely on a steady flow of consumer dollars. Coordinated boycotts, ethical purchasing campaigns, and disruption of supply chains through grassroots actions directly impact their profits. Financial pressure forces accountability where public appeals fail.

Empower Communities to Demand Transparency
Demand that corporations disclose political contributions, lobbying efforts, and tax practices. Grassroots advocacy and legal actions can push for stronger regulations to curb corporate influence. Educating communities about these practices empowers collective action against systemic corruption.

How Corporations and Politicians Have Enslaved Us

Billionaires have built an empire of control by forging an unholy alliance between corporations and politicians, effectively enslaving us to their greed. Through this powerful duo, they manipulate every facet of society, economy, governance, and even our daily choices, while ensuring their wealth and influence remain untouchable. The tools of their domination are as insidious as they are pervasive, leaving the rest of us scrambling to survive under the weight of their systemic exploitation.

Corporations are the enforcers, wielding their unchecked power to dictate everything from wages to rents, prices to policies. They hoard resources, destroy small businesses, and turn essential needs like housing, healthcare, and education into profit streams. Meanwhile, politicians, bought and paid for with campaign donations and lobbying dollars, craft legislation that solidifies this power dynamic. Tax loopholes for billionaires, anti-union laws, and gutted social safety nets are not accidents, they are the calculated results of this corruption.

We are trapped in a cycle that benefits the few while crushing the many. Jobs that once provided stability now barely cover the cost of living. Families are forced into debt for basic needs. And when people demand change, they're met with propaganda that blames immigrants, the poor, or anyone else but the billionaires and politicians orchestrating the oppression.

This system thrives on division and disempowerment, keeping us too busy fighting each other or struggling to make ends meet to challenge their control. But it doesn't have to be this way. Recognizing their tactics is the first step toward breaking these chains. Only by dismantling the billionaire-corporate-political complex can we reclaim our freedom and build a society that prioritizes people over profits. The time for opposition is now, before their chains tighten any further.

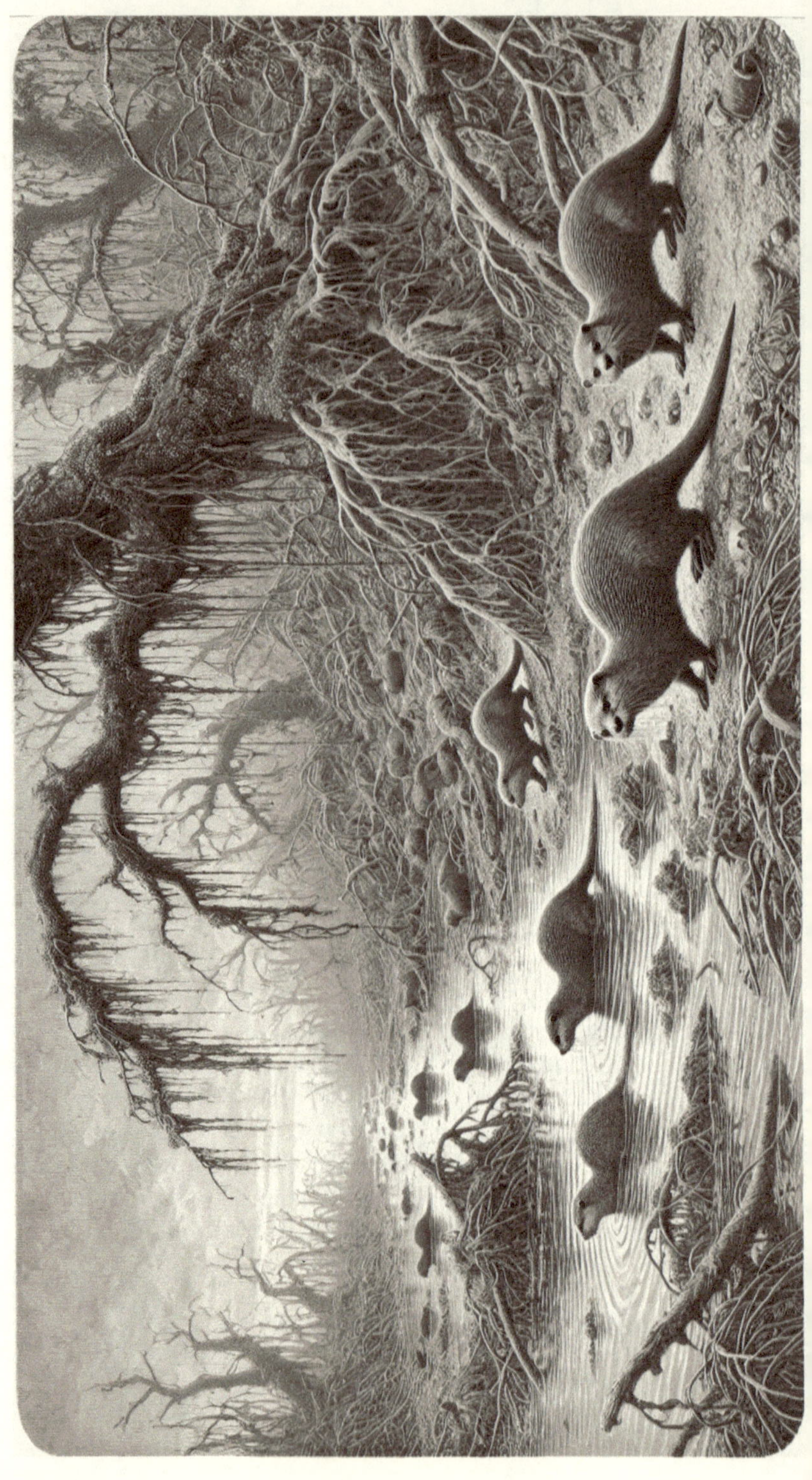

Chapter 5
The Ecological Devastation of Wealth

Billionaires are the architects of ecological collapse. Their relentless pursuit of profit has transformed the planet into a resource to be exploited, with no regard for the destruction left in their wake. Rainforests, once vast and teeming with life, are razed for monoculture plantations that strip the soil bare and displace entire communities. Oceans are emptied of marine life by industrial-scale fisheries, leaving barren waters and collapsing ecosystems. Rivers, the lifeblood of countless communities, are poisoned by industrial runoff, turning what was once pure and sustaining into toxic channels of disease. These actions are not accidents or unfortunate byproducts of human progress; they are deliberate choices, made with full knowledge of the harm they cause.

This scale of destruction is not natural. It is a distortion of humanity's relationship with the environment, driven by greed so vast and unrelenting it has become a force unto itself. Billionaires commodify the natural world, reducing forests, oceans, and entire ecosystems to profit margins. In doing so, they strip the earth of its intrinsic value, treating it as disposable in their pursuit of ever-expanding wealth. This commodification is profoundly destructive, not just ecologically but morally, eroding any sense of responsibility for the planet or its inhabitants.

At the same time, these billionaires cloak themselves in the language of sustainability. They sponsor climate summits, launch "green" initiatives, and donate to environmental organizations. Their public personas are carefully curated to project an image of concern and responsibility. Yet behind the scenes, they continue to invest heavily in the very industries driving climate collapse. Fossil fuels, deforestation, and mining for rare earth minerals underpin their wealth, even as they tout their commitment to renewable energy and conservation.

This hypocrisy is most evident in the tech billionaires who position themselves as saviors with solutions like electric vehicles and solar panels. While these innovations are touted as progress, they come at a tremendous cost. The mining of lithium, cobalt, and other minerals needed for these technologies devastates landscapes, poisons water supplies, and exploits workers, particularly in the Global South. These so-called solutions do not address the root causes of the climate crisis; instead, they perpetuate the same extractive logic under a different guise.

Through this performative greenwashing, billionaires profit from both sides of the crisis. They reap the rewards of causing climate disasters and then turn around to sell false solutions to the very problems they created. Their philanthropic gestures, far from being altruistic, serve as tools to deflect criticism and maintain their control. Each donation, each tree-planting campaign, each headline about their "sustainability efforts" is a carefully calculated move to obscure their complicity in the destruction of the planet.

This strategy extends beyond actions to the narratives they create. Billionaires normalize ecological collapse as an unavoidable consequence of progress. Rising sea levels, disappearing species, and scorched landscapes are reframed as the cost of advancement, necessary sacrifices for the march of innovation. This is the essence of sane-washing: taking the grotesque and presenting it as rational. Through media outlets they own and politicians they fund, they flood public discourse with language that dulls the urgency of the crisis. Phrases like "sustainable growth" and "market solutions" sanitize the destruction, making it seem less like a catastrophe and more like a technical problem with a technical fix.

This narrative is deeply insidious. By reframing environmental devastation as inevitable, it saps the collective will to resist. If rising sea levels and poisoned rivers are simply the cost of progress, then why fight back? If billionaires' innovations are the only path forward, then who has the right to question them? This logic creates a sense of despair, a belief that the world is too broken to save and that opposition is futile. And billionaires thrive on despair, knowing that a demoralized population is far easier to control.

The psychological impact of these narratives cannot be overstated. Billionaires manipulate public consciousness, reshaping reality to serve their interests. They dominate the conversation, drowning out alternative visions of the future and ensuring that their version of progress is the only one that seems plausible. The grotesque becomes normalized, the unnatural becomes inevitable, and the possibility of change feels distant, if not impossible.

But the connections between environmental destruction and economic oppression cannot be ignored. The same greed that devastates ecosystems also deepens inequality. Vulnerable communities bear the brunt of environmental collapse, displaced by rising seas, poisoned by industrial waste, and left to suffer as billionaires retreat to their fortified mansions. The climate crisis is not just an ecological issue; it is a justice issue. Those who have contributed the least to the problem suffer the most, while those responsible profit without consequence.

This interconnectedness underscores the urgency of opposition. Environmental justice is inseparable from the fight against billionaires. Their greed fuels the destruction of both the planet and the social systems meant to protect it. Their wealth insulates them from the consequences of their actions, while the rest of the world pays the price. Fighting for the environment means fighting against the structures that allow billionaires to exploit it with impunity.

The planet is not a commodity to be consumed and discarded. It is a shared home, a place of intrinsic value that sustains all life. Billionaires, in their relentless pursuit of profit, have turned this home into a battleground, stripping it of its sanctity and leaving destruction in their wake. But this battle is not yet lost. Recognizing the narratives they use to maintain control is the first step in reclaiming power. Refusing to accept their lies, their greenwashing, and their sane-washing is an act of defiance. And from that defiance, a movement can grow, one that prioritizes the planet over profit, justice over greed, and a livable future over the temporary comforts of billionaires.

The environmental devastation caused by billionaires extends far beyond the destruction of ecosystems, it reshapes the fabric of communities, nations, and global stability. The relentless extraction of resources and the commodification of nature do not occur in a vacuum. They are part of a larger system that prioritizes short-term profits over long-term survival, leaving billions of people to contend with the fallout. This is not an accident or an unfortunate side effect of progress; it is a deliberate choice made by those who see the world as nothing more than a balance sheet to exploit.

Billionaires are often shielded from the consequences of their actions, retreating to luxury compounds and disaster-proof bunkers as climate disasters become more frequent and severe. They live in a world insulated from rising seas, polluted air, and water shortages, a world built on the backs of those who are left to suffer the consequences. As coastal communities are displaced, small farmers lose their land to desertification, and entire towns are poisoned by industrial waste, billionaires continue to amass wealth, secure in their privilege.

This inequality is most starkly evident in the Global South, where resource extraction is concentrated. Corporations backed by billionaire investors exploit these regions with impunity, displacing indigenous peoples, destroying biodiverse habitats, and leaving poisoned landscapes in their wake. Mining for rare earth minerals, essential for the tech-driven "green" solutions billionaires champion, often results in toxic runoff that devastates local water supplies. For the communities affected, the environmental costs are immediate and devastating, entire ecosystems collapse, livelihoods are lost, and public health deteriorates. These are not isolated incidents but symptoms of a global system that sacrifices the vulnerable to feed the insatiable greed of the powerful.

The hypocrisy of billionaires extends to their response to the climate crisis they have fueled. In the face of rising criticism, they have adopted a dual strategy of greenwashing and technocratic overreach. On one hand, they invest heavily in PR campaigns to present themselves as environmental saviors, funding reforestation projects or pledging net-zero emissions for their companies by some distant future date. On the other hand, they propose grandiose technological solutions that conveniently align with their financial interests, geoengineering schemes, carbon capture technologies, or speculative investments in renewable energy infrastructure. While these initiatives are framed as bold steps toward sustainability, they rarely address the root causes of environmental degradation. Instead, they reinforce the same systems of extraction and exploitation that created the crisis.

Consider the narrative surrounding carbon offsets, a favorite tool of billionaires seeking to greenwash their activities. By investing in projects that claim to reduce or absorb emissions elsewhere, they absolve themselves of responsibility for their continued reliance on fossil fuels and high-carbon industries. Yet many of these offset programs are riddled with flaws. Forests earmarked for preservation are often double-counted or poorly managed, and the promised reductions in emissions frequently fail to materialize. Worse, these programs displace indigenous communities, depriving them of access to their ancestral lands in the name of environmental protection. This is not sustainability, it is exploitation dressed in green.

The distortion of environmental narratives goes even deeper. Billionaires and their corporate allies have mastered the art of reframing systemic failures as individual shortcomings. In their telling, the climate crisis is not the result of unchecked industrialization, resource extraction, or runaway consumption, it is the fault of everyday people who drive cars, use plastic straws, or fail to recycle diligently. This deflection shifts the burden of responsibility away from the true culprits and onto the public, fostering guilt and paralysis while allowing billionaires to continue their destructive practices unchecked.

This strategy is particularly evident in the push for individual consumer choices as a solution to climate change. While personal responsibility has its place, it is a drop in the ocean compared to the emissions generated by industries controlled by billionaires. Just 100 companies are responsible for 71% of global greenhouse gas emissions, yet the focus remains on whether individuals are using reusable bags or turning off their lights. This deliberate misdirection serves to obscure the systemic nature of the crisis and protect the interests of those who benefit from it.

Even as billionaires exploit the environment, they profit from the disasters they create. Climate change has become an investment opportunity for the ultra-wealthy, who fund disaster response technologies, insurance schemes, and even privatized water supplies. As droughts worsen and clean water becomes scarcer, billionaires position themselves to profit from the commodification of this most basic necessity. Similarly, as wildfires rage and hurricanes grow more destructive, they invest in resilient infrastructure projects and luxury disaster-proof housing. For them, the climate crisis is not a threat but a chance to expand their wealth and influence.

The psychological impact of these practices is profound. The pervasive sense of inevitability they cultivate, through media narratives, political lobbying, and corporate messaging, erodes public confidence in the possibility of change. This despair is not incidental; it is a deliberate tool of control. When people believe that environmental collapse is inevitable, they are less likely to demand accountability or fight for systemic change. Billionaires thrive on this resignation, using it to maintain their grip on power while continuing their destructive practices.

But the climate crisis is not inevitable, and the narrative of despair can be countered with a narrative of opposition. Communities around the world are already fighting back, from indigenous activists defending their lands against deforestation to grassroots movements demanding corporate accountability. These efforts, though often overlooked, offer a blueprint for how to challenge the billionaire-driven systems of exploitation. They remind us that change is not only possible but essential.

Environmental justice is inseparable from social and economic justice. The fight to protect the planet is also a fight to dismantle the structures that allow billionaires to profit from its destruction. It is a fight to recognize the intrinsic value of the natural world, to honor the rights of those most affected by environmental degradation, and to demand accountability from those responsible. This is not just a moral imperative but a survival necessity.

Reclaiming the planet requires a fundamental shift in how we think about progress, growth, and prosperity. It demands that we move away from the extractive, profit-driven model championed by billionaires and toward a system rooted in sustainability, equity, and respect for the earth's limits. This is not a simple task, but it is a necessary one. It begins with rejecting the narratives that billionaires have constructed and replacing them with a vision of a world where people and planet take precedence over profit.

The battle against ecological collapse is not just about saving the environment, it is about reclaiming humanity's future. Billionaires have shown us what their version of the future looks like: a world of fortified compounds for the wealthy, surrounded by the wreckage of a planet pushed beyond its limits. But there is another future possible, one built on collective action, shared responsibility, and a deep respect for the interconnectedness of all life. It is up to us to fight for that future and to ensure that the billionaires who have brought us to the brink of collapse are held accountable for their actions.

This fight will not be easy, but it is a fight worth waging. The planet is not a resource to be exploited; it is a home to be protected. And while billionaires may have the money and influence to shape the world in their image, they do not have the power to silence the voices of those who refuse to accept their vision. Opposition begins with recognizing the lies, exposing the hypocrisy, and demanding a future where life, not profit, is the ultimate measure of success.

The Machinery of War: Greed, Control, and the Military-Industrial Complex

The billionaires who shape our world are not just exploiters of natural resources; they are warlords in suits, architects of destruction who profit from suffering on an unimaginable scale.

The military-industrial complex, the vast network of weapons manufacturers, private military contractors, and defense corporations, exists not to preserve peace but to perpetuate war, because war is profitable. And the billionaires who fund and control these industries thrive on conflict.

Every war, every military intervention, every new contract signed to produce tanks, missiles, or drones is a financial boon for those at the top. The same billionaires who claim to be champions of innovation and economic growth are, in reality, dealers of death, growing richer while entire nations burn. Violence, displacement, and devastation are not unintended consequences; they are the business model.

The United States spends more on its military than the next ten countries combined. In 2023, military expenditures reached a staggering $877 billion, a number that dwarfs spending on education, healthcare, and climate action. While millions struggle with medical debt, housing insecurity, and failing infrastructure, taxpayer money is funneled into the pockets of Lockheed Martin, Raytheon, Boeing, and Northrop Grumman, all companies that exist solely to profit from war.

This is not security. This is theft on a grand scale. The U.S. Department of Defense is the single largest institutional polluter on the planet. It consumes more fossil fuels than most countries, producing more carbon emissions than 140 nations combined. The production, transport, and use of military equipment, from fighter jets to aircraft carriers, leaves an environmental impact so vast that even the most destructive private industries cannot compare.

Yet, when climate activists call for meaningful change, we are told to carpool, stop using plastic straws, or switch to paper bags. Meanwhile, the military burns an estimated 269,000 barrels of oil per day, an ecological catastrophe carefully omitted from mainstream climate discourse.

The irony is grotesque: the very entities that claim to defend civilization are, in reality, hastening its collapse. The U.S. military has poisoned over 175,000 square miles of land and water, rendering entire regions uninhabitable. Burn pits in Iraq and Afghanistan released toxic fumes that have caused lifelong health issues for veterans and civilians alike. Nuclear weapons testing has left vast swaths of the planet irradiated and unlivable. Depleted uranium shells contaminate battlefields for generations, leading to birth defects and cancers in war-torn regions. And yet, the architects of these atrocities face no consequences. Instead, they are rewarded with lucrative contracts, government bailouts, and total immunity from accountability.

The violence billionaires unleash abroad does not stay contained to distant battlefields. The weapons, technologies, and methods of suppression perfected in foreign conflicts are brought home and used against the very citizens who funded them. The militarization of the police in the United States is a direct product of the military-industrial complex. Armored vehicles, riot gear, and high-powered weaponry once reserved for war zones now patrol American streets. Police departments receive billions of dollars in military equipment under the 1033 Program, turning local law enforcement into occupying forces.

The results are catastrophic. Police killings have skyrocketed. In 2023 alone, U.S. law enforcement officers killed over 1,200 people, the highest number in recorded history. Black and brown communities bear the brunt of this brutality, living under the constant threat of state violence, while corporations and billionaires ensure that justice is never served. At the same time, domestic violence, mass shootings, and organized hate crimes are at record highs. The connection is clear: a society built on war abroad will inevitably become a battlefield at home. The normalization of violence as a tool of control seeps into every institution, shaping the way power is enforced.

For over a century, Posse Comitatus has served as a legal barrier preventing the U.S. military from being used against its own citizens. Established in 1878, the Posse Comitatus Act was designed to prevent the federal government from deploying the Army or Air Force as a domestic police force, recognizing the dangers of military power being turned inward. But now, there are increasing calls to dismantle this safeguard.

In recent years, politicians and corporate-backed think tanks have floated the idea of using the military to quell civil unrest, a terrifying escalation that threatens the very foundations of democracy. In 2020, during nationwide protests against police violence, the Trump administration deployed federal agents and military forces in multiple cities, signaling a chilling shift toward military enforcement of domestic policy. In 2023, reports surfaced that legislators were considering repealing or weakening Posse Comitatus, citing concerns over crime and "domestic extremism." But who defines extremism? The same billionaires who profit from oppression? The same corporations funding war and surveillance?

If Posse Comitatus falls, the consequences will be immediate and devastating. The military will no longer be constrained to foreign battlefields; it will be deployed against striking workers, against climate activists, against marginalized communities demanding justice. The same tactics used to suppress dissent in occupied nations will be unleashed on American soil. This is not speculation. This is the logical next step in the billionaire class's consolidation of power.

The narrative we are sold, the lie that terrorism comes from outsiders, from rogue states, from distant enemies, is a carefully constructed diversion from the truth. The true architects of terror are not hiding in caves or plotting from the shadows. They own skyscrapers, investment firms, defense companies, and media conglomerates. They are the billionaires who manufacture war, profit from suffering, and manipulate global systems to ensure their own enrichment at the cost of millions of lives. They are the ones funding military coups to protect their investments. They are the ones lobbying for endless wars to keep their factories running. They are the ones extracting wealth from dying ecosystems while preaching sustainability. They do not need bombs or guns to seize power, they already own the governments that wield them.

We are told that war is inevitable. That the economy depends on military spending. That there is no alternative to the endless cycle of conflict, oppression, and destruction. These are lies, crafted, refined, and repeated by those who benefit from our silence. But war is not inevitable. Oppression is not natural. Ecological collapse is not the cost of progress. These are all deliberate choices, choices made by billionaires who see the world as their playground, the people as their workforce, and the earth as nothing more than a disposable resource. To resist this system is not just an environmental fight. It is a fight for the very soul of humanity.

It begins with rejecting the billionaire class's narratives, refusing to believe their lies about security, progress, and innovation. It continues with building solidarity across movements, uniting environmentalists, labor unions, and anti-war activists in a common cause. It demands direct action, not passive petitions. Protests, strikes, and mass mobilization are the only tools that have ever forced change.

And above all, it requires an unwavering belief that another world is possible. A world not ruled by billionaires and war profiteers, but by the people who refuse to be controlled, refuse to be exploited, and refuse to be silent. Because silence is exactly what they want. And that is why we will not give it to them.

And those telling us to sit down and shut up? The media isn't some noble fourth estate holding power to account, it's corporate garbage, bought and paid for by billionaires and their "special" interests. Internet news isn't independent by default, and podcasts, newsletters, and so-called alternative voices are just as compromised. More influencers than ever are quietly bankrolled by the far right, and those who aren't are often selling out because that's where the money flows. Truth doesn't pay, but propaganda does. And so, the cowardice spreads, like cockroaches darting through the cracks, avoiding the light, whispering the lies they're paid to repeat.

Meanwhile, they push endless wars abroad and divisions at home, keeping people distracted while the real theft happens in plain sight. Because it's not just about money, it's about power, about keeping people too exhausted, too angry at each other, too desperate to see who's actually pulling the strings. They tell us we can't have nice things, but the truth is, there job is to make sure we never will. Well don't we have news for them... The tide is turning, the illusion is cracking, and the reckoning they never saw coming is already at their doorstep.

Draw or list what a world at peace looks & feels like below:

The river had once been a source of life. It ran through the heart of the town, nourishing the land and sustaining the people who lived along its banks. Families gathered there for picnics, children played in its waters, and local fishermen relied on its bounty to make a living. But that was before the factories came, before the billionaire turned the river into a dumping ground for the waste produced by his industries. Now, the river was a shadow of its former self, a murky, toxic expanse that poisoned rather than nourished. The air around it carried a foul odor, and the water shimmered with an unnatural sheen.

For the families who still depended on the river, there was no escaping its impact. Their crops withered, their livestock sickened, and their children developed mysterious illnesses that no doctor could adequately explain. The river had become a symbol of the billionaire's control, a vivid reminder of how his pursuit of profit had devastated the community.

The teenager, now a young adult, could no longer ignore the toll the river was taking. Their earlier discoveries about the billionaire's erasure of history and manipulation of narratives had opened their eyes to the interconnectedness of economic and ecological oppression. The same greed that had driven families into poverty was also destroying the environment, and it was the most vulnerable who suffered the most.

Driven by a growing sense of purpose, the teenager began organizing with peers around the issue of environmental justice. They met in living rooms, libraries, and the few remaining green spaces in town, sharing stories of how the river's contamination had affected their lives. These gatherings were marked by a mix of anger and determination. Anger at the billionaire who had caused so much harm, and determination to fight back.

The group decided to start by gathering evidence. Armed with notebooks, cameras, and water-testing kits, they documented the river's contamination and its impact on the surrounding community. They took photographs of the dead fish that lined the riverbanks, recorded videos of the oily slicks that floated on the water's surface, and collected testimonies from residents about the illnesses and hardships they had endured. Each piece of evidence was a weapon in their fight against the billionaire's narrative of progress and prosperity.

But documenting the damage was only the beginning. The group knew they needed to raise awareness beyond their small town if they were to have any hope of holding the billionaire accountable. They launched a social media campaign, sharing their findings under the hashtag #PoisonedByGreed. The posts quickly gained traction, drawing attention from environmental activists, journalists, and everyday people who were horrified by the images and stories coming out of the town.

As the campaign gained momentum, the group organized a protest at the gates of the billionaire's largest factory. They stood in the shadow of the towering facility, holding signs that read "Clean Our River" and "Your Greed Kills." The protest drew a crowd, with residents, activists, and even some former factory workers joining the demonstration. For the first time in years, the community felt a sense of solidarity, a shared belief that they could challenge the billionaire's control.

The billionaire's response was predictably ruthless. Security guards were deployed to break up the protest, and local media, owned by the billionaire, ran stories painting the demonstrators as disruptive troublemakers. But the protest had achieved its goal: it had drawn national attention to the issue. Environmental organizations and independent journalists began investigating the river's contamination, uncovering decades of negligence and cover-ups.

For the teenager, the fight was as much about reclaiming the narrative as it was about cleaning the river. The billionaire had spent years convincing the town that their suffering was an unfortunate but necessary trade-off for economic development. He had framed the factory as a symbol of progress and the river's contamination as an unavoidable side effect of industry. But the teenager and their group were determined to challenge that

140

narrative, to show that the destruction of the river was not progress but greed in its most grotesque form.

The group's efforts began to pay off. A coalition of environmental organizations filed a lawsuit against the billionaire, accusing him of violating environmental laws and endangering public health. The lawsuit drew widespread attention, forcing the billionaire to issue a public statement denying the allegations and touting his commitment to sustainability. But the statement rang hollow, especially in the face of the overwhelming evidence presented by the coalition.

The fight for the river was far from over, but the teenager and their peers had already achieved something remarkable. They had shown the community that opposition was possible, that the billionaire's power was not as absolute as it seemed. The poisoned river, once a symbol of the billionaire's control, had become a rallying point for defiance and hope.

But the struggle was not without its challenges. The billionaire's lawyers fought tooth and nail to discredit the lawsuit, using every tactic at their disposal to delay proceedings and intimidate witnesses. Local officials, many of whom were financially tied to the billionaire, refused to take a stand, insisting that the issue was out of their hands. And the group faced constant surveillance and harassment, with members receiving anonymous threats warning them to back down.

Despite these obstacles, the teenager remained resolute. They knew that the fight for the river was about more than just environmental justice, it was about challenging the systems that allowed billionaires to exploit both people and the planet with impunity. They saw the river's contamination as a microcosm of a larger issue, a reflection of the greed and corruption that permeated society.

The teenager also understood that their fight was part of a broader movement. They connected with activists from other communities facing similar struggles, sharing strategies and resources. They learned about towns fighting against toxic landfills, indigenous groups defending their lands from deforestation, and coastal communities battling rising seas. These connections reinforced their belief in the interconnectedness of economic and ecological oppression and inspired them to keep pushing forward.

The group's next move was to organize a town hall meeting, inviting residents to share their stories and discuss solutions. The meeting was held in a local church, its pews filled with people from all walks of life. One by one, residents stood up to speak, their voices trembling with emotion as they recounted the ways the river's contamination had affected them. A farmer described how his crops had failed year after year. A mother tearfully shared how her child had developed severe asthma after playing near the river. An elderly man, who had worked at the factory for decades, spoke of his regret at not speaking out sooner.

The stories were heartbreaking, but they also galvanized the community. By the end of the meeting, there was a renewed sense of purpose and a commitment to take further action. The group drafted a list of demands, including the immediate cleanup of the river, compensation for affected residents, and stricter regulations to prevent future contamination. They presented the demands to local officials, backed by the signatures of hundreds of residents.

The teenager knew that real change would take time, but they also knew that the fight was worth it. The river, once a source of life, had become a symbol of greed and exploitation. But it could also become a symbol of opposition and renewal. The community's struggle to reclaim the river was about more than just cleaning the water, it was about reclaiming their dignity, their agency, and their future.

The community realized that enough was enough. The fight for the river was just the beginning, but the magnitude of the problem demanded something larger. It wasn't enough to clean a single waterway or hold one billionaire accountable; they needed to dismantle the systems that allowed such destruction to flourish in the first place. The teenager and their group understood that their small town was a microcosm of a global issue, an issue rooted in unchecked greed, environmental neglect, and a disregard for human dignity.

142

It was time to think and act bigger. The group began organizing on a regional scale, connecting with other communities impacted by industrial greed. They envisioned a network of activists, scientists, and citizens who could pool resources, share knowledge, and amplify each other's voices. They planned protests targeting not just local factories but the corporate headquarters of the billionaire's empire. They launched a campaign to demand legislative change, aiming to pass stricter environmental regulations and expose the corrupt ties between corporations and politicians.

The teenager knew they were up against enormous power, but they also knew that collective action could topple even the most entrenched systems. It was time to challenge the billionaire's control over their lives and redefine what progress truly meant, for the river, the community, and the planet.

War for the Survival of the Planet & Humanity's Will

The poisoned river stands as a vivid, localized reminder of a far more pervasive truth: billionaires are not just profiteers exploiting opportunities; they are active agents of destruction, operating with a deliberate disregard for the cost their greed exacts on the planet and its people. The scale of their harm transcends isolated incidents like this one polluted waterway. Instead, it reveals a global pattern of ecological devastation that threatens the very foundation of life on Earth. Billionaires, in their relentless pursuit of profit, are akin to demons sent to test humanity's will to survive, pushing the limits of what the planet and its people can endure.

The river's toxic transformation mirrors countless other ecological crises unfolding worldwide. Vast rainforests, which once pulsed with life and regulated the planet's climate, are incinerated or clear-cut to make way for cattle grazing and palm oil plantations owned by billionaire-backed conglomerates. Oceans, a source of life for billions, are stripped bare by industrial fishing fleets while vast garbage patches float on their surfaces. Communities dependent on these ecosystems are left to grapple with collapsing livelihoods and poisoned environments, while billionaires insulate themselves from the consequences in their private compounds and climate-proof retreats.

This devastation is no accident, it is an engineered consequence of a system that prioritizes profit above all else. Billionaires actively shape policies, fund propaganda, and undermine regulations to ensure their destructive practices remain legal and lucrative. They bankroll think tanks that promote narratives of "sustainable growth," selling a vision of progress that justifies endless extraction and exploitation. Even their public gestures of environmental concern, such as sponsoring clean energy initiatives or launching green tech startups, are often shallow attempts to mask their complicity in driving the very crises they claim to address.

The poisoned river is emblematic of how these billionaires operate: exploit, extract, destroy, and deflect. The damage is localized, but the strategy is global. Whether it's water contaminated by industrial runoff, air polluted by unchecked emissions, or entire regions rendered uninhabitable by climate change, the story is the same. Vulnerable communities bear the brunt of the destruction, while billionaires amass ever more wealth, profiting even from the disasters they cause. They position themselves as indispensable, problem-solvers equipped with the capital and innovation to lead humanity through the crises they created. Yet their "solutions" often deepen existing inequalities and reinforce their stranglehold on power.

This is not a war on nature, it is a war for the sanctity of the planet, and humanity stands at a crossroads. Billionaires embody a greed so monstrous that it defies reason, eroding the fragile balance of life on Earth for the sake of temporary profit. Framing them as mere opportunists is insufficient; they are far more dangerous. Their actions reveal an almost otherworldly capacity to rationalize destruction, as if they see themselves as separate from the ecosystems they exploit. Like demons in myth, they exist to test humanity's resolve, to see if we will succumb to despair and inaction, or if we will rise to reclaim the planet.

The river's story is not unique, but it serves as a microcosm of the broader struggle. For every poisoned waterway, there are displaced farmers, dying coral reefs, and forests silenced by chainsaws. Each of these tragedies is connected by the same forces of greed and exploitation. Billionaires have turned the planet into a battleground, where their insatiable pursuit of wealth collides with humanity's right to a livable future. The stakes are as high as they have ever been: survival versus collapse, justice versus greed, life versus destruction.

Yet, within this dire reality, there is also an opportunity. The poisoned river, and the community's fight to reclaim it, demonstrates that opposition is possible. It begins with recognizing the pattern of exploitation, exposing the billionaires who perpetuate it, and rejecting the narratives that frame their actions as inevitable or necessary. It continues with collective action, movements that challenge their power, demand accountability, and offer alternative visions of progress rooted in sustainability and equity.

146

The fight is not just against ecological collapse but against the system that allows it to happen. It is a fight for justice, for dignity, and for the right to live in harmony with the planet rather than in subjugation to those who would exploit it. The billionaires may hold the reins of power, but they are not invincible. Their control relies on the belief that they are untouchable, that their wealth and influence place them beyond reproach. Shattering this illusion is the first step toward change.

The poisoned river and the billions of lives affected by similar crises across the globe remind us that this is a battle worth fighting. The Earth, once a source of abundance and interconnected life, has been turned into a battlefield where the forces of greed wage war against the very systems that sustain us. But humanity has a choice. The billionaires' greed is not inevitable, it is a constructed system that can be dismantled. Their narratives of progress and inevitability are not immutable truths, they are lies designed to keep us passive.

This war for the sanctity of the planet demands courage, imagination, and a refusal to accept the grotesque as normal. It calls on humanity to rise above the despair billionaires cultivate and to act with the urgency the crisis demands. Opposition must be fierce and unyielding, for the alternative is unthinkable: a future in which rivers run toxic, forests fall silent, and the Earth itself becomes a barren wasteland. The time to act is now, not just for the river or the town it once sustained, but for the survival of all life on this shared, fragile planet.

Politicians Are Useless: Return Power to the People

Let's face it: politicians are no longer the representatives of the people, they're the mouthpieces of corporations and billionaires who bankroll their campaigns. The result? A system riddled with corruption, gridlock, and policies that serve the wealthy while leaving the rest of us behind. It's time to bypass this broken system and return power to the people through direct action. The solution lies in technology: imagine voting, decision-making, and civic participation streamlined through an app, accessible, secure, and democratic.

Here's how it works: an app can allow communities or townships to vote on local issues, make decisions, and engage directly in governance without waiting for politicians to act, or, more accurately, to stall. The app could provide verified voting by phone, instant access to town hall-style discussions, and real-time updates on community initiatives. Instead of relying on elected officials to advocate for us, we advocate for ourselves, empowered by the simplicity of digital democracy.

To make this vision a reality, all we need is one township or community willing to pilot the program. A small-scale test would allow us to refine the technology, demonstrate its effectiveness, and build trust in the process. Once proven, the model can scale up, bringing grassroots, tech-driven democracy to more regions.

Selling this concept up the food chain is simple: emphasize efficiency, accessibility, and cost savings. Instead of bloated political machines draining resources, communities gain direct control, transparency, and empowerment. The time has come to bypass the useless, corrupt intermediaries and let people govern themselves. With a simple app and the will to act, we can show the world what true democracy looks like, no politicians required. Have a vision and change will follow.

Draw or make a list of what outrage looks & feels like below:

Chapter 6
Demons of Greed
A Moral Reckoning

It is not hyperbole to suggest that billionaires may be, in the most literal sense, evil demons. The unrelenting greed, destruction, and moral void that define their existence are so extreme that conventional human explanations fail to fully capture their behavior. What if they are not merely deeply flawed humans but something else entirely, something beyond the realm of human comprehension, embodying the kind of malevolence usually reserved for myth and scripture? To explore this possibility is not only intellectually provocative but morally necessary. For in a world where billionaires exist as untouchable forces of destruction, we are faced with a profound moral crisis that demands resolution.

Let us first consider the defining characteristics of demons across various cultural and religious traditions. Demons are often depicted as beings whose sole purpose is to corrupt, deceive, and destroy. They thrive on chaos and suffering, feeding off the pain and despair of others while remaining untouched by it themselves. Now compare this to the actions of billionaires: their wealth and power are derived directly from systems that exploit and oppress billions of people while devastating the planet. They operate with impunity, hoarding resources, manipulating governments, and shaping public narratives to justify their insatiable greed. Like demons, they seem to exist outside the moral framework that governs ordinary people, their actions untethered from any sense of responsibility or empathy.

Their relationship to suffering is particularly damning. Billionaires accumulate wealth by perpetuating conditions of inequality, poverty, and environmental destruction. They profit from systems that trap billions in cycles of despair, extracting the labor and resources of the many to fuel their insatiable consumption. Worse, they not only ignore the suffering they cause but often frame it as necessary or inevitable. How is this different from the demonic act of convincing humanity that suffering is unavoidable, that their torment is part of some grand cosmic order? It is a chilling parallel, one that forces us to question whether their actions can truly be considered human.

The scale of their harm defies comprehension. Billionaires possess more wealth than entire nations, yet their impact on the world is overwhelmingly destructive. They destabilize democracies by funding politicians and think tanks that prioritize corporate interests over public good. They perpetuate ecological collapse, turning rainforests into barren wastelands and poisoning oceans and rivers in the pursuit of profit. They commodify basic human needs, healthcare, housing, education, and drive them out of reach for millions. These are not merely acts of greed; they are acts of systemic, calculated harm that strip dignity, agency, and life from vast swaths of humanity. Such behavior is not just inhuman, it borders on the supernatural.

The psychological manipulation employed by billionaires adds another layer to the argument. They have mastered the art of sane-washing, reframing their destruction as progress and their greed as virtue. Through media empires, PR campaigns, and political puppets, they craft narratives that obscure their culpability and normalize the grotesque. Mass deportation centers become "security measures," poisoned rivers are dismissed as "unfortunate trade-offs," and climate collapse is sold as the cost of advancement. This level of deceit, deliberate, pervasive, and corrosive, is eerily reminiscent of the demonic ability to twist reality itself. Billionaires do not merely thrive in the systems they exploit; they distort the world to make their exploitation seem rational, even necessary.

But perhaps the most damning evidence of their potential demonic nature is their detachment from humanity. Billionaires live lives so removed from ordinary existence that they may as well occupy a different plane of reality. They build fortresses to shield themselves from the consequences of their actions: luxury bunkers to escape climate disasters, private islands to avoid accountability, and sprawling estates far removed from the communities they exploit. Their wealth insulates them from the suffering they create, allowing them to perpetuate harm without ever confronting its impact. This detachment is not merely a privilege; it is a profound moral failing. To act without regard for the harm one causes is to embody the very essence of evil.

Moreover, their inability, or refusal, to recognize the inherent wrongness of their existence further supports the demonic comparison. Billionaires often justify their wealth and power as the result of hard work, innovation, or merit. This narrative ignores the systemic exploitation that underpins their fortunes and the immense harm they inflict on others. They position themselves as saviors, launching philanthropic ventures and technological solutions that serve more as PR stunts than genuine attempts to address the crises they have caused. Their philanthropy, while lauded by the media, often reinforces the very systems of inequality they claim to fight. It is a sinister cycle: create problems, profit from the solutions, and emerge as a hero. Such self-serving logic mirrors the demonic trait of perpetuating harm while masquerading as a force for good.

The existence of billionaires is both a policy failure and a moral crisis that humanity must address. Each billionaire is not just a product of economic systems gone wrong but a reflection of the moral decay we have allowed to fester, until the rot is so vast that almost no sunlight remains to expose it. There is no rational justification for their obscene wealth, no ethical framework that can reconcile their accumulation of resources with the suffering it creates. In a world where billions struggle for clean water, basic healthcare, and enough food to survive, the presence of even a single billionaire is an affront to both justice and human decency. Their wealth is not earned, it is stolen, extracted from the labor of others and the destruction of the planet. To tolerate their existence is to accept a world where greed triumphs over justice, where individual excess outweighs collective well-being.

But addressing this moral crisis requires more than critique, it demands action. Billionaires wield enormous power, not only through their wealth but through the systems they control. They have the resources to shape laws, influence elections, and dominate public discourse. Dismantling their power will require a collective effort, one that challenges the narratives they have constructed and reclaims the moral high ground. It means exposing their actions for what they are: not progress, but destruction; not innovation, but exploitation; not virtue, but vice.

Humanity must reject the idea that billionaires are simply successful individuals who have worked harder or been smarter than everyone else. This narrative serves only to legitimize their existence and obscure the harm they cause. Instead, we must recognize them as active agents of harm, forces of destruction whose continued existence threatens the survival of the planet and the dignity of humanity. Whether they are literal demons or simply the human embodiment of greed, their actions are undeniably evil, and their power must be dismantled.

But addressing this moral crisis requires more than critique, it demands action. Billionaires wield enormous power, not only through their wealth but through the systems they control. They have the resources to shape laws, influence elections, and dominate public discourse. Dismantling their power will require a collective effort, one that challenges the narratives they have constructed and reclaims the moral high ground. It means exposing their actions for what they are: not progress, but destruction; not innovation, but exploitation; not virtue, but vice.

Humanity must reject the idea that billionaires are simply successful individuals who have worked harder or been smarter than everyone else. This narrative serves only to legitimize their existence and obscure the harm they cause. Instead, we must recognize them as active agents of harm, forces of destruction whose continued existence threatens the survival of the planet and the dignity of humanity. Whether they are literal demons or simply the human embodiment of greed, their actions are undeniably evil, and their power must be dismantled.

The moral urgency of this issue cannot be overstated. Billionaires' unchecked greed has created a world where inequality deepens, ecosystems collapse, and hope becomes increasingly scarce. Their very existence poses a question of values: Do we prioritize the well-being of humanity and the planet, or do we continue to worship at the altar of wealth? Choosing the latter is not only a failure of morality but an existential gamble. We stand at a crossroads, and the stakes are nothing less than the survival of the

Earth and the integrity of our shared humanity. If we do not act now to confront this moral crisis, we may find ourselves living in a world where the worst impulses of the few have extinguished the future for the many.

The Greed Virus and the Insanity of Tolerating Billionaires 1 Second Longer

We have long known that extreme wealth and power breed sociopathy. Psychological studies repeatedly show that those in financial and political control exhibit reduced empathy, increased entitlement, and a dangerous detachment from ordinary life. The hoarding of wealth, particularly in a world where billions suffer, is not success or ambition; it is a mental illness, a sickness of the soul, a pathological greed that defies logic and morality. Yet, instead of treating billionaires as the dangerous individuals they are, we celebrate them. We idolize them. We let them dictate policy, write laws, and shape the world in their image. Why? Why do we not recognize them for what they truly are, patients in need of treatment, if not outright containment? Instead, we are gaslit, told hoarding is normal, that these men, almost always men, are the pinnacle of human achievement rather than the embodiment of a failing system. We are not a healthy society; we are an insane one, spiraling into a sickness so deep it has warped our perception of morality, justice, and decency.

There is no time left to waste. This is not a crisis for future generations, it is a moral emergency now. Every day billionaires exist unchecked, more lives are lost, ecosystems collapse, and the path to justice becomes steeper. The billionaire class thrives on delay, deflection, and scapegoating. They shift blame onto the poor, immigrants, and those fighting for justice. They buy politicians who keep the system rigged. They fund propaganda convincing people that their suffering is their own fault. And all the while, we wait, wait for Congress to act, for courts to rule, for a miracle that will never come. We wait as if justice will be delivered, when in reality, it has always been ours to take.

Let us be absolutely clear: billionaires are not victims of a broken system. They are its architects. They are not just the beneficiaries of policy failures; they *are* the policy failures, the human embodiment of everything that has gone wrong with modern civilization. Their wealth is not earned; it is extracted, siphoned from the labor of the working class, stolen from the earth's resources, funneled upward through loopholes and corruption. And what do they give back? Nothing. They do not build societies; they dismantle them. They do not create prosperity; they hoard it. They do not innovate; they monopolize. Their philanthropy is a sham, a tax write-off, a performance designed to pacify the masses while they tighten their grip on the world's resources. To tolerate their existence is to accept a world where suffering is not just inevitable but engineered.

And what are we told in response? That we should be grateful. That these men, these living incarnate demons of greed, have somehow *earned* their power. That the system works, that anyone can achieve their level of success if they just work hard enough. This is the greatest lie ever sold. The very structure of our economy is designed to ensure that wealth remains concentrated in the hands of the few. The billionaire class does not rise through talent or ingenuity; they rise through exploitation, inheritance, and the active suppression of competition. They manufacture scarcity where there should be abundance. They create crises and then sell solutions at a premium. They drive wages down, drive rent up, poison the environment, and then convince us that this is simply the way things must be. It is not. It never was.

The most disturbing aspect of billionaire rule is how they have weaponized perception itself. Through media ownership, political donations, and cultural influence, they have reshaped reality to suit their needs. They have convinced entire nations to fight among themselves, to see each other as enemies rather than recognizing the true oppressors. They have turned suffering into an individual moral failing rather than a systemic design. And most insidiously, they have made us believe that their downfall is impossible. That they are too powerful, too entrenched, too untouchable. This is the final trick of the billionaire class: to convince the people that resistance is futile. But it is not.

156

History shows us that no empire lasts forever, and no tyrant remains unchallenged. The billionaire class is not an immovable force; they are a fragile elite propped up by illusions, by the belief that their wealth grants them divine right. But their power is an illusion, one that shatters the moment we refuse to comply, the moment we stop accepting their narratives, the moment we decide to take back what has been stolen from us. We must reject the idea that billionaires are a necessary evil. They are not necessary, and they are not merely evil, they are existential threats to democracy, to justice, to life itself. If we do not act, they will continue to consolidate power, to reshape society into a digital feudalism where they rule as untouchable lords and we serve as disposable serfs.

The road ahead will not be easy. We are not just fighting wealth; we are fighting a system built to protect it. Laws favor the rich, politicians are bought, and courts serve billionaires. We cannot wait for elections or incremental reforms. The billionaire class has made their intentions clear, and we must respond. Organize, educate, disrupt. Boycott their corporations, divest from their industries, build alternatives. Expose their corruption, challenge their monopolies, and refuse to participate in their system.

Most of all, we must recognize that we are the change we have been waiting for. No one is coming to save us. No politician, no judge, no institution will fix what has been thoroughly broken. It is up to us. We, the people, hold the power. We always have. The billionaire class may have wealth, but we have numbers. History has shown time and again that when the many rise against the few, the few always fall.

There is no justification for their existence. There is no moral argument for their continued hoarding of wealth while billions suffer. There is no reason to wait. The time for debate is over. The time for action is now. If we do not stand against this grotesque perversion of wealth and power, if we do not dismantle this system with everything we have, then we have already surrendered. But if we rise, if we organize, if we refuse to comply with a world that serves only the interests of billionaires, then we can reclaim what is rightfully ours. Justice. Dignity. A future worth believing in.

Billionaires are the disease. We are the cure.

Can We Really Wait 1 Second Longer Before We Act?

One million seconds = 11 days, 13 hours, 46 minutes, and 40 seconds
One billion seconds = 31 years, 8 months, 16 days, 9 hours, 46 minutes, and 40 seconds

Perspective:
If you had one dollar per second, you'd have a million dollars in about 11.5 days.
If you had one dollar per second, you'd have a billion dollars in about 31.7 years.

This difference demonstrates the staggering scale of a billion compared to a million, a billion is 1,000 times larger.

Average American Salary
According to recent data, the average U.S. annual salary is around $60,000.
This translates to approximately $5,000 per month, $1,154 per week, or $164 per day (assuming a 365-day year).

Broken Down by Time
Per hour: ~$28.85 (assuming a standard 40-hour workweek).
Per minute: ~$0.48.
Per second: ~$0.008 (or 0.8 cents per second).

Time Required to Earn $60,000
At $0.008 per second, 7.5 million seconds, or 87 days.

So, in one second, the average American worker makes about 0.8 cents, while a billionaire can make hundreds or thousands of dollars per second, further highlighting the vast wealth disparity.

TYCOON
TYCOON
TYCOON

Time passed, as it always does, but not without consequence. The teenager and their group had fought valiantly, organizing protests, drafting demands, and rallying the community. Yet, despite their efforts, the system proved relentless, its roots too deep, its reach too vast. The billionaire's empire, once a distant specter, had seeped into every corner of their lives, reshaping the town into something unrecognizable. What began as a fight for the river had become a battle for their very existence, a battle they were losing.

The group's momentum faltered. The town hall meetings grew smaller, the protests quieter. The billionaire's lawyers tied up their demands in endless litigation, while his media outlets painted them as radicals, troublemakers, enemies of progress. The teenager watched as hope drained from the faces of their neighbors, replaced by resignation. The river, once a rallying cry, became a bitter reminder of their failure. It still flowed, dark and poisoned, a testament to the cost of waiting too long to act.

The system tightened its grip. Smart devices, once optional, became mandatory. Jobs were automated or outsourced, leaving the townsfolk dependent on gig work dictated by algorithms. The teenager's father, once proud of his factory job, now spent his days chasing tasks on an app that tracked his every move. Their mother, once a skilled seamstress, now completed mindless microtasks for pennies, her hands trembling from exhaustion. The family's access to basic services, heat, water, even food, was tied to their compliance score, a number they couldn't see but felt in every restriction.

The streets grew quieter, not out of peace, but fear. Surveillance cameras and drones patrolled every corner, their unblinking eyes recording every step, every word. The teenager's older sibling, who had fought so fiercely, was gone, not just from the town, but from the digital world. Their profile deactivated, their access revoked, they had become a non-person, a ghost in the machine.

The teenager wondered if they had found the Unlinked or if the system had simply erased them.

And still, the teenager waited. For what? A sign? A spark? Permission? They didn't know anymore. The system had become too powerful, too pervasive. It wasn't just the river or the factory or the billionaire, it was everything. The schools, the shops, the parks, even the homes. The town no longer belonged to its people. It belonged to the algorithm, to the tycoon, to the faceless entity that controlled it all. But the teenager couldn't give up. Not yet. They had seen the cracks in the system, the quiet resistance hidden beneath forced smiles and automated pleasantries. They had heard the whispers of the Unlinked, faint but persistent. And they knew, deep down, that an object in motion stays in motion until it is stopped. The system was in motion, relentless and unchecked. But so were they. The fight wasn't over. It couldn't be. Not yet.

The apathy of the other citizens was perhaps the hardest to bear. Many had simply given up, too exhausted by the constant barrage of demands, restrictions, and surveillance to fight back. They had been worn down by the system's strategy of shock and awe, a relentless onslaught of changes, each more destabilizing than the last. One day it was a new tax on water usage; the next, a mandatory update to their home security systems. The rules shifted constantly, leaving no time to adapt, no room to breathe. It was designed to keep them off-balance, to keep them too tired to resist.

The teenager saw it for what it was: a calculated effort to ensure obedience. The system didn't just demand compliance; it manufactured it. By throwing everything at them, the kitchen sink, the walls, the ceiling, it created a state of perpetual exhaustion. And exhaustion bred apathy. Why fight when the fight seemed impossible? Why resist when resistance only brought more punishment?

The town no longer belonged to its people. It had been reshaped, reprogrammed, optimized, not for those who lived within its borders, but for the faceless entity that controlled it. The tycoon's empire had grown silently at first, slipping into their homes, their streets, their routines. It had arrived as convenience, as innovation, as the future made real. But now, the future felt like a trap, and the walls of their world were closing in.

The smart devices in their homes were no longer luxuries; they were necessities. Thermostats that adjusted themselves, refrigerators that tracked their groceries, cars that refused to start if the algorithm detected a payment issue. There was no opting out. Even their jobs were assigned by the system, applications filtered by unseen hands, promotions and terminations dictated by a score that no one fully understood. It wasn't enough to work hard. It wasn't enough to be qualified. The algorithm had to approve of you. And if it didn't, you ceased to exist, not physically, but digitally, which in this world was just as damning.

People whispered about the old days, when a person's worth was measured by their labor and character. Now, it was measured in data points, in behavioral predictions, in patterns of compliance. The town had become a petri dish for the tycoon's ambitions, an experiment in total control where every citizen was a test subject. The schools, once places of learning, had become training centers for a future none of them had chosen. The students weren't taught to think critically, but to function within the system. They weren't educated; they were programmed.

For the teenager, this realization came slowly, then all at once. They had watched their parents accept it, had seen their older sibling try to fight it and disappear into the void of deactivated profiles and revoked access. Their father, once a factory worker, now spent his days performing gig work dictated by an app, the same app that penalized him for too many bathroom breaks. Their mother, once a seamstress, now took on microtasks, endless streams of mindless labor fed to her through a screen, each paying just enough to keep them afloat but never enough to break free.

The streets were quiet, eerily so. Crime had been eliminated, not because people had become more just, but because the system had no tolerance for deviation. The cameras caught everything. A wrong step, a wrong word, and suddenly the opportunities disappeared. No notice. No explanation. Just silence where there had once been access. It was a world of precision-engineered obedience, where the fear of exclusion was stronger than any physical threat.

The town still looked the same on the surface. The shops were open, the lights glowed warmly in the evenings, the parks remained well-kept. But it was all an illusion. The stores no longer accepted cash. The parks were monitored by drones. The homes had no locks that couldn't be overridden remotely. Doors could be sealed shut at the whim of the system, access revoked for reasons unknown, and those inside would simply vanish from society. The people had learned not to ask questions, not to step out of line, because they had seen what happened to those who did.

The teenager began noticing the gaps in the illusion, the quiet resistance hidden beneath forced smiles and automated pleasantries. A store clerk hesitating before scanning a customer's chip, a delivery driver who lingered just long enough to whisper a warning before disappearing into the night. They began hearing rumors, stories of people who had found a way out, who had slipped through the cracks of the system and disappeared into the shadows. These whispers were faint, almost imperceptible, but they carried a glimmer of hope. The teenager clung to them, even as the digital cage tightened around them.

It started with small acts of defiance. The teenager began to question the rules, to test the boundaries of the system. They refused to use the recommended apps for their schoolwork, opting instead for outdated textbooks they found in the library. They avoided the surveillance cameras by taking long, winding routes through the town, memorizing blind spots and dead zones. They even started to notice patterns in the algorithm's behavior, times when it seemed to lag, moments when it overlooked minor infractions. These small victories gave them a sense of control, a feeling that they were more than just a data point in the tycoon's grand experiment.

But the system was relentless. It adapted, learned, and tightened its grip. The teenager's school performance began to suffer as the algorithm flagged their refusal to conform. Their parents received notifications about their "non-compliance," and the family's access to certain services was restricted. The teenager's father was assigned fewer gigs, their mother's microtasks became more demanding, and the family's financial stability began to crumble.

The system was punishing them, not just for the teenager's actions, but for their collective resistance. The teenager's older sibling had warned them about this. Before they disappeared, they had spoken of a network, a hidden community of people who had rejected the system entirely. They called themselves the Unlinked, and they lived off the grid, surviving on the fringes of the digital world. The teenager had dismissed it as a fantasy at the time, but now they began to wonder.

Could the Unlinked be real? And if they were, could they offer a way out?

The first step was finding them. The teenager knew it wouldn't be easy. The system monitored every communication, every movement, every transaction. To reach the Unlinked, they would have to become invisible, to erase their digital footprint and disappear without a trace. It was a daunting task, but the alternative was unthinkable. The teenager couldn't spend the rest of their life as a cog in the tycoon's machine, their every action dictated by an algorithm. They had to try.

They started by disconnecting from the system as much as possible. They stopped using their smart devices, opting for analog alternatives wherever they could. They avoided public spaces, sticking to the shadows and relying on their knowledge of the town's blind spots. They even began to experiment with hacking, using old devices and pirated software to bypass the system's controls. It was risky, but the teenager was determined. They had nothing left to lose.

As the days turned into weeks, the teenager began to notice strange things. The system seemed to be watching them more closely, as if it sensed their defiance. Notifications became more frequent, more insistent. Their family's access to essential services was further restricted, and their parents grew increasingly desperate. The teenager knew they were running out of time. If they didn't find the Unlinked soon, the system would crush them completely.

Then, one night, it happened. The teenager was hiding in an abandoned warehouse on the outskirts of town, trying to access an old server they had heard might contain information about the Unlinked. As they worked, they heard a noise behind them. They turned, expecting to see a drone or a security bot, but instead, they saw a figure, a person, dressed in dark clothing and wearing a mask. The figure stepped forward, holding up a hand in a gesture of peace.

"You're looking for the Unlinked," the figure said, their voice low and steady. "You've been searching for us. But you need to understand, once you join us, there's no going back. The system will never stop hunting you. Are you ready for that?"

The teenager hesitated. They thought of their family, of the life they were leaving behind. But they also thought of the future, a future where they were free to think, to act, to live on their own terms. They nodded.

"I'm ready," they said.

The figure smiled beneath their mask. "Then follow me."

And with that, the teenager stepped into the shadows, leaving the digital cage behind. They didn't know what lay ahead, but for the first time in a long time, they felt a spark of hope.

Action: Rising TIDE

The teenager stood in the dim light of an abandoned warehouse, their breath visible in the cold air. Around them, a small group of peers huddled, their faces a mix of fear and determination. These were the ones who hadn't given up, the ones who still believed in the possibility of resistance. They had all felt the weight of the system's oppression, the constant surveillance, the relentless demands, the suffocating control. But tonight, they were done waiting. Tonight, they would act.

The teenager had spent weeks studying the principles of Rising TIDE: Target, Inspire, Disrupt, Empower. It was a framework they had learned from whispers of the Unlinked, a way to fight back against systems that seemed invincible. Now, they shared it with the group, their voice steady despite the adrenaline coursing through their veins.

"We can't take on the whole system at once," they began, "but we can chip away at it. We start by targeting the tycoon's profits. If we hurt his bottom line, we hurt his power."

The group leaned in, their eyes sharp with focus. One by one, they brainstormed ideas. A coder suggested hacking into the algorithms that controlled gig work, creating glitches that would

168

slow productivity. A former factory worker proposed organizing a boycott of the tycoon's products, urging the town to stop buying from his stores. Another member, a graphic designer, offered to create propaganda, flyers, videos, and memes that would expose the tycoon's greed and inspire others to resist.

"We need to inspire people," the teenager said, picking up the thread. "They've been beaten down for so long, they've forgotten what it feels like to fight back. We remind them. We show them they're not alone."

The group nodded, their resolve hardening. They planned a series of small, symbolic acts of defiance, graffiti on surveillance cameras, messages of hope scrawled on walls, even a flash mob in the town square. Each act was designed to disrupt the system's control and empower others to join the resistance.

"Disruption is key," the teenager continued. "We need to throw the system off balance. If we can create enough chaos, even for a moment, we can show people that the tycoon's power isn't absolute."

The coder grinned. "I can create a botnet to flood the tycoon's servers with fake data. It won't take him down, but it'll slow him down."

"And we can organize a digital strike," another member added. "If enough people refuse to use his apps, even for a day, it'll send a message."

The teenager felt a surge of hope. This was it, the beginning of something bigger. They knew the risks. The tycoon's reach was vast, his resources limitless. But they also knew that every system had its weaknesses, and every tyrant could be toppled.

"Finally," they said, "we empower others. This isn't just about us. It's about everyone who's been crushed by this system. We show them that resistance is possible, that they have power too."

The group spent hours refining their plans, their energy building with each new idea. They knew the road ahead would be dangerous, but they also knew they had no choice. The town was dying, suffocating under the weight of the tycoon's greed. If they didn't act now, there might not be a town left to save.

As the meeting ended, the teenager looked around at their peers. They were just a handful of people, up against an empire. But they were determined. They were angry. And they were ready to fight. The town remained under the tycoon's oppressive grip, but for the first time in a long time, there was a spark of defiant hope. The fight was far from over, but it had begun. And that was enough.

The next few days were a blur of activity. The coder worked tirelessly, infiltrating the tycoon's systems and planting seeds of disruption. The graphic designer's propaganda began appearing overnight, bold, striking images that called out the tycoon's exploitation and urged the town to rise up. The former factory worker organized a small but growing boycott, spreading the word through whispers and coded messages.

The teenager took on the role of coordinator, ensuring that each action was timed perfectly to maximize impact. They knew that the tycoon's algorithms would adapt quickly, so they had to stay one step ahead. Every glitch, every act of defiance, was a calculated move in a larger game.

One night, the group gathered again in the warehouse to assess their progress. The coder reported that the tycoon's servers were struggling under the weight of the botnet attack. The graphic designer shared stories of townsfolk who had seen the propaganda and begun to question the system. The factory worker smiled as they recounted how the boycott was gaining traction, with more and more people refusing to buy from the tycoon's stores.

But the teenager knew this was only the beginning. The tycoon would retaliate, and when he did, it would be swift and brutal. They had to be ready.

"We need to keep pushing," the teenager said, their voice firm. "We've disrupted his systems, but we haven't broken them. We need to inspire more people, to show them that they can fight back too."

The group agreed, their determination unwavering. They planned their next moves carefully, knowing that each action carried greater risk. But they also knew that the stakes were too high to back down now. As they left the warehouse that night, the teenager felt a strange mix of fear and exhilaration. They were just a handful of people, up against an empire. But they were fighting back. And for the first time in a long time, they felt like they had a chance.

The town remained under the tycoon's oppressive grip, but the spark of defiant hope was growing. The fight was far from over, but they weren't giving up. And that was enough, for now.

The Cost of Inaction and the Spark of Defiance

The story of the teenager and their small band of resisters is not just a tale of rebellion; it is a mirror held up to our own world, reflecting the consequences of inaction and the necessity of defiance. The teenager's journey, from passive observer to active resistor, echoes the struggle we all face in a society increasingly dominated by the unchecked greed of billionaires and the systems they control. Their fight is our fight, and their story is a warning: the cost of waiting is too high.

The first part of the chapter, *Inaction*, lays bare the devastating consequences of delay. The teenager and their community fought valiantly, but their efforts were fragmented, their momentum faltering under the weight of the billionaire's relentless onslaught. The system, designed to exhaust and destabilize, wore them down with its constant barrage of demands, restrictions, and surveillance. The apathy of the townsfolk, born of exhaustion and fear, became the tycoon's greatest weapon. Why resist when resistance seems futile? Why fight when the fight only brings more punishment? This is the insidious logic of oppression, and it is a logic we must reject.

And that is how we end up where we are, the second part of the chapter, *Digital Cage.* Is it any different than America 2025?

The third part, *Action: Rising TIDE*, offers a glimmer of hope. The teenager, now joined by a small group of peers, begins to apply the principles of resistance: Target, Inspire, Disrupt, Empower. They target the tycoon's profits, inspire their community to rise up, disrupt the systems of control, and empower others to join the fight. It is a blueprint for resistance, a reminder that even the most entrenched systems can be challenged. But it is also a reminder that resistance is not easy. It requires courage, determination, and a willingness to risk everything. The teenager and their group are just a handful of people, up against an empire. But they are fighting back, and in their defiance, we see the possibility of change.

This duality, inaction and action, despair and hope, lies at the heart of the story. It is a reflection of our own world, where the greed of billionaires has created a moral crisis that demands resolution. The tycoon in the story is not just a fictional villain; he is the embodiment of a system that prioritizes profit over people, power over justice, and greed over humanity. His wealth is not earned; it is extracted, siphoned from the labor of the many to fuel the excesses of the few. His power is not legitimate; it is manufactured, maintained through manipulation, coercion, and fear. And his existence is not inevitable; it is a choice, one that we, as a society, have allowed to persist for far too long.

The story of the teenager is a call to action, a reminder that we cannot wait for someone else to save us. The billionaire class will not relinquish their power willingly; it must be taken from them. This is not a fight for the faint of heart, but it is a fight we cannot afford to lose. The stakes are nothing less than the survival of our planet and the dignity of humanity.

And so, we return to the image of the otters standing up to the billionaire demon. It is a powerful metaphor, one that speaks to the strength, courage, and lack of choice we have in opposing fascism and the unending greed of the mentally ill billionaires. The otters, small and seemingly powerless, refuse to bow to the demon's might. They fight not because they believe they will win, but because they know they must. Their defiance is not just an act of resistance; it is an act of survival. And in their struggle, we see our own.

The billionaire class thrives on our inaction. They rely on our exhaustion, our apathy, our belief that resistance is futile. But the story of the teenager and the image of the otters remind us that resistance is not just possible, it is necessary. We cannot wait for a savior; we must be the saviors. We cannot wait for justice; we must take it. And we cannot wait for change; we must create it.

Chapter 7
The Inevitability of Opposition

The problem is not new. The cycles of exploitation, wealth consolidation, and the suffocation of popular dissent have defined the structure of civilization for millennia. What is new is the scale. Never before have so few controlled so much while disguising their theft as progress. Never before have they had the technological tools to surveil, manipulate, and crush resistance before it even begins. But history does not move in a straight line. Every empire built on exploitation has imagined itself eternal, only to fall when the people it depended on to fuel its machinery refused to play their part. The opposition to oligarchy is not just possible, it is inevitable.

The political institutions that once held even the illusion of democracy have rotted from within. Congress does not represent the people; it represents the billionaires and corporate interests that fund its campaigns. The presidency is a revolving door between financial elites, war profiteers, and corporate yes-men. The courts, once a theoretical check on the excesses of power, have become an enforcement arm for those who would strip the people of their rights and hand the country over, piece by piece, to the highest bidder. The very concept of representative democracy has become a farce, a thin veneer of legitimacy stretched over the machinery of theft. This system cannot be reformed because it was designed to resist reform. It cannot be salvaged because it was built to protect the wealthy from accountability.

Expecting change from within this system is not just naïve, it is a waste of time we no longer have. The billionaire class has waged war on the people, the planet, and the very concept of fairness itself. And for too long, they have dictated the terms of engagement. They have controlled the avenues of resistance, ensuring that any attempt at reform is swallowed by bureaucracy, kneecapped by legal barriers, or co-opted into meaningless spectacle. They have bought the media that shapes the public consciousness, ensuring that the idea of revolution is framed as lunacy, while the slow and methodical destruction of human rights is labeled "inevitable market correction." They have convinced generations that resistance is futile and that they are too powerful to overthrow. This is their greatest weapon: not force, not wealth, but the illusion of inevitability.

But history tells a different story. Power is never as secure as it seems. The most brutal empires, the most entrenched ruling classes, the most unshakable institutions, all of them fell when the people they oppressed refused to comply. And we are at that moment again. The billionaire class believes it has built a world where no opposition can touch them. But the systems they rely on, the markets, the surveillance networks, the labor forces they exploit, are not as stable as they believe. The harder they tighten their grip, the closer they come to collapse.

The old forms of resistance, strikes, mass protests, political revolutions, remain powerful, but in an era where surveillance is all-encompassing, where media narratives are controlled, and where movements are infiltrated before they can even begin, resistance must evolve. And it is evolving. The future of opposition is not in playing by their rules, but in building new systems that render them obsolete. The billionaire class controls the financial institutions? Decentralized finance removes them from the equation. They manipulate elections? Direct, blockchain-based governance eliminates the need for representatives who can be bought. They hoard and control the distribution of resources? AI, ethically guided and collectively managed, can optimize resource allocation to eliminate scarcity itself.

This is not utopian speculation. The tools already exist. Blockchain technology enables decision-making that is transparent, incorruptible, and decentralized, allowing for governance that bypasses the gatekeepers of wealth and power. AI, if freed from the grip of corporations that seek to use it for profit and control, can be used to optimize food distribution, automate essential services, and eliminate the inefficiencies deliberately built into capitalist scarcity models. The billionaire class fears these technologies not because they are dangerous, but because they have the potential to make them irrelevant.

We have seen this pattern before. Every time the people have been backed into a corner, crushed under the weight of oppressive systems, they have innovated their way out. When feudal lords hoarded wealth and land, the printing press gave the people knowledge, undermining the Church and the nobility. When industrial barons reduced workers to near-slavery, the labor movement forced the creation of unions, safety regulations, and the eight-hour workday. Every system that has attempted to consolidate absolute control has faced the inevitability of its own collapse.

Today is no different. The ruling class would like us to believe that they are invulnerable, that their grip on power is absolute. They believe that because they own the media, they own the narrative. That because they own the politicians, they own the law. That because they own the means of production, they own the future. But they do not own us.

Throughout history, grassroots movements have dismantled oppressive systems by refusing to play by their rules. The Civil Rights Movement defied legal oppression not through official channels, but through direct action, community organizing, and mass noncompliance. The anti-colonial movements of the 20th century drove out imperial powers that had ruled for centuries, not by asking for permission, but by forcing the issue through relentless resistance. The fall of the Berlin Wall, the Arab Spring, the ongoing resistance movements across the world today, all of these prove one thing: No system, no matter how powerful, is immune to the will of the people.

The tools of resistance have evolved, but the spirit remains the same. The same forces that toppled kings, dismantled empires, and rewrote history are moving now. And despite all the surveillance, despite all the control, despite all the wealth hoarded by the few, they cannot stop it.

The future will not be ruled by billionaires. It will not be shaped by corrupt politicians, by corporate greed, by the machinery of destruction that has dictated history for too long. The systems that allowed them to rise are crumbling. The post-representative revolution is already underway. Decision-making is shifting away from centralized power structures and toward localized, transparent, collective governance. The people are reclaiming their agency, not just politically, but economically, socially, technologically.

This is not a question of if. It is a question of when.

The old world is dying. The billionaire class knows this. That is why they are fighting so desperately to maintain their grip, why they are pushing for greater control, more surveillance, more authoritarianism. Because they see what is coming. They see that their time is running out.

Opposition is inevitable because humanity does not tolerate oppression forever. And the moment they fear most is approaching. The moment where the people stop believing in their illusions, stop accepting their rules, and realize that they are the many, and the billionaires are few.

And when that moment comes? The floodgates will break.

Stop the Steal

The so-called golden age of the American middle class wasn't some miraculous outcome of free markets or capitalist ingenuity. It was engineered through deliberate policies, massive public investment, and a level of economic intervention that would make today's billionaires weep. From the 1940s through the 1960s, high taxes on the rich, strong labor unions, and a government that actually invested in its people created an economy where regular people could afford homes, education, and retirement.

During World War II, the government poured money into industry, infrastructure, and innovation, creating millions of jobs and laying the foundation for decades of economic prosperity. And after the war, instead of letting the ultra-rich hoard everything, policy decisions ensured that prosperity was shared. The top tax rate on the wealthiest Americans was over 90% under FDR and Eisenhower. Over 35% of workers were unionized, giving them real bargaining power. The GI Bill gave millions of veterans access to higher education and homeownership. Government-funded infrastructure projects built roads, schools, and hospitals.

The result? A booming middle class, rising wages, and the longest period of economic stability in American history. One worker's salary could support a family. College was affordable. Retirement was an actual *thing* people could do. But there was a catch. This prosperity was largely limited to white men. Black Americans were systematically locked out of the best benefits of the New Deal and the post-war boom. Women were pushed out of the workforce and expected to return to the home. LGBTQ+ people were criminalized and erased. The system worked, but only for those it was designed to serve.

And then, as marginalized groups began demanding their fair share, the ruling class panicked. Black Americans wanted real civil rights. Women wanted economic and social equality. LGBTQ+ people wanted to live openly without persecution. And that? That was unacceptable to the people at the top, because if everyone got a piece of the pie, there'd be less left for them. The backlash was swift and brutal.

In 1971, corporate lawyer Lewis Powell wrote what would become one of the most important documents in modern American history, the Powell Memo. It was a blueprint for corporate America to take back control and make sure the economic policies of the 1940s–1960s never happened again. The memo outlined how corporations needed to:

- Take over universities and shape public education to favor corporate interests
- Buy up media outlets to control the narrative
- Pack the courts with pro-business judges
- Destroy labor unions to stop workers from having any power
- Convince people that taxing the rich was bad and deregulation was good

And it worked. By the time Ronald Reagan took office in 1981, the war against the middle class was in full swing. Reagan slashed the top tax rate from 70% to 28%, effectively handing trillions to the richest Americans. He waged an all-out war on labor unions, crushing their power and setting the stage for decades of wage stagnation. He deregulated industries, making it easier for corporations to buy elections, gut social programs, and consolidate their wealth.

This was the beginning of the greatest wealth transfer in history, not from the rich to the poor, but from everyone else to the top 1%. Over the past four decades, more than $50 trillion has been siphoned from the working and middle class into the hands of billionaires.

And as the ultra-rich grew even wealthier, they rigged the system to keep it that way. Bill Clinton gutted welfare and deregulated Wall Street. George W. Bush gave massive tax cuts to the wealthy and started forever wars. Barack Obama bailed out the banks instead of homeowners. Donald Trump passed another multi-trillion-dollar tax cut for the ultra-rich. Every administration since Reagan has operated within the same neoliberal framework, one where corporations and billionaires write the rules, and the government exists only to serve them.

Now, we're at the breaking point. The top 1% owns more wealth than the bottom 90% combined. Real wages have barely budged in 40 years while corporate profits hit record highs. Housing, healthcare, and education are luxuries instead of basic rights. And now, the billionaire class isn't satisfied with just hoarding wealth, they want to cement their control forever.

Enter Project 2025, a far-right plan to dismantle what little remains of American democracy. It is a direct continuation of the Powell Memo and Reaganomics, designed to strip away civil rights, gut social programs, and push the U.S. back into a 19th-century economic order where billionaires rule unchecked.

A national abortion ban is already in the works. Women's rights are being rolled back, and some conservatives are openly questioning whether women should even have the right to vote. Voting rights are under full-scale assault, gerrymandering, voter suppression laws, and Supreme Court rulings have already stripped millions of people, especially Black, Brown, and Indigenous voters, of their voice in elections. LGBTQ+ rights are being systematically targeted, with anti-trans laws and "Don't Say Gay" bills spreading across the country.

And let's not forget that the billionaires pulling these strings don't care about "America" or "patriotism." They're more than happy to sell off the country to the highest bidder. While they fearmonger about "foreign threats," they outsource jobs, sell land, and make deals with authoritarian regimes in the Middle East and China. Because at the end of the day, they only care about profit.

If democracy actually worked the way it should, this fascist nightmare wouldn't have a chance of winning elections. But thanks to decades of:
- Gerrymandering
- Voter purges
- Supreme Court rulings gutting voting rights
- The Electoral College tilting power toward conservatives

The non-insane, jus regular greedy and corrupt, party has to win by millions of votes just to break even. In the last presidential election alone, millions of votes were thrown out, gerrymandered, or outright suppressed. If those votes had counted, the entire political landscape would be different. Instead, the oligarchy is tightening its grip, and they aren't even trying to hide it anymore. We are at a crossroads.

Either we continue down this road, where billionaires and corporations own everything, where wages stagnate while profits soar, where basic rights are stripped away, where democracy is a distant memory, or we fight back.

Fighting back means refusing to accept the lies we've been sold about trickle-down economics, deregulation, and "free markets." It means restoring voting rights, taxing the ultra-rich, breaking up monopolies, and reinvesting in public goods. It means refusing to let the billionaire class continue its war on workers, the environment, and democracy itself.

And it starts with recognizing this is not an accident. This is a heist. The people who stole our wealth, crushed our democracy, and sold us out are not going to stop unless we stop them. History shows that change does not come from waiting. It comes from action. And if we don't act now, we're not just losing democracy. We're losing the future.

Fair is Fair

There are no big ideas anymore, no moon shots, no grand visions of a better world. The billionaire class has seen to that, hoarding not just wealth but imagination itself. They've turned progress into a commodity, innovation into a weapon, and fairness into a relic of a bygone era. So, if they won't play fair, neither will we. We're coming to take what's ours, and we're not asking permission.

Some of the only power we have left is to make this new America as unpleasant for them as they have made it for us. Stop smiling at Nazis, or anyone you don't know is on your side. None of this "kill them with kindness" nonsense, none of this "you catch more flies with honey than with vinegar." Flies are pests, and so are they. And as for civility? Unbelievable. Unbelievable and yet so typical. Is it civil to steal our bodily autonomy, to police our bodies, our voices, our thoughts? Is it civil to murder babies in wars waged for profit, to deny basic human services like healthcare and education? No. Absolutely not. But we are awake now, and present. We are the big idea. Today, tomorrow, we are the change we have been waiting for.

So, no, we will not be nice anymore. We will not play by their rules, because their rules are rigged. We will not extend courtesy to those who would strip us of our dignity. We will not offer kindness to those who thrive on cruelty. Fair is fair, and if they won't give us fairness, we'll take it. We'll take it by disrupting their systems, by exposing their lies, by refusing to comply with their demands. We'll take it by organizing, by resisting, by fighting back. And we'll take it by making their world as uncomfortable as they've made ours.

Because here's the truth: they don't deserve our kindness. They don't deserve our patience. They don't deserve our silence. What they deserve is accountability. And if they won't give it to us willingly, we'll take it by force. Fair is fair.

The Flood of Liberation

The weight of years spent under the billionaire's shadow was heavy, but something had shifted. The young adult stood before the gathered community, their voice steady despite the fear that gripped them all. The town, once bound by silence and compliance, was beginning to stir. The meetings had grown larger, the whispers had become words, and now those words had turned into plans. They spoke of futures, of alternatives, of an end to the reign of invisible masters. The billionaire's presence still loomed, an omnipresent specter in their streets, their screens, their systems. But the people were no longer afraid to name it.

The nights were long, filled with hushed conversations and the soft glow of encrypted screens. What had begun as isolated pockets of defiance had grown into something far more formidable, a network beyond the tycoon's control. Blockchain, once a tool of speculation, had been reclaimed as a means of governance, a way to ensure no single hand could hold absolute power. AI, once wielded against them, now helped allocate resources with efficiency and fairness. They had turned the tools of the system against their creators, weaving new structures from the ruins of the old.

The speeches came like waves, the young adult's words rolling over the crowd with the force of something undeniable. They spoke of labor movements that had been erased from history, of ancestors who had fought and bled for dignity. They spoke of what the system had taken, homes, futures, voices, and what it could never take: their will to resist. And above all, they spoke of the dam. The monstrous structure that had come to symbolize the billionaire's grip on the land, the blockade that held back not just the river, but their collective power. The dam had to fall. It was time.

The night was thick with tension as they moved. The plan had been perfected over months, calculated to the second. Drones watched from above, scanning for deviations, anomalies. But they had learned to hide in plain sight, their movements choreographed with machine-like precision. The surge came not in reckless violence, but in cold, unrelenting precision. The first detonation sent a crack through the dam's foundation, and the crowd held its breath. Then another. And another. And then, the roar of water as the first breach was made. The dam, a symbol of everything they had endured, began to crumble.

The flood came, not just of water, but of catharsis, of liberation. The billionaire's empire did not fall that night, but it had been wounded. The young adult stood at the river's edge, watching as the barriers collapsed, as something ancient and free reclaimed its course. The fight was not over. There would be others to take the billionaire's place, new threats cloaked in different guises. But tonight, they had won something real. Not just the river, not just their land, but the undeniable proof that they could fight, and that they could win.

The young adult, now a leader within their community, gathered the disparate voices of the town under a shared vision of resistance. The meetings were held in the shadow of the billionaire's looming presence, a specter that haunted every conversation, every plan. The tone was Southern Gothic, with elements of horror, the kind of horror that comes not from the supernatural, but from the all-too-real monstrosity of unchecked greed. The billionaire's influence was everywhere, in the drones that patrolled the skies, in the algorithms that dictated their lives, in the dam that choked the river. But the people were no longer silent. They had found their voice, and they were ready to use it.

The narrative built as the community adopted decentralized technologies to coordinate their actions. Blockchain, once a tool of speculation and greed, was reclaimed as a means of governance. It became a ledger of transparency, a way to ensure that no single hand could hold absolute power. AI, once wielded against them, now helped allocate resources with efficiency and fairness. They had turned the tools of the system against their creators, weaving new structures from the ruins of the old. The descriptions were rich and atmospheric, blending the eerie remnants of the old system with the hopeful, almost sacred energy of the new.

The young adult delivered a rallying speech to the community, invoking both the past struggles of labor movements and the future possibilities of collective technology-driven governance. Their words were interspersed with dreamlike visions of the dam, the symbol of corporate and political control, beginning to crack. They spoke of the ancestors who had fought and bled for dignity, of the futures that had been stolen, and of the will to resist that could never be taken. The dam had to fall. It was time.

The community launched their symbolic attack on the dam, using a mix of coordinated direct action and technological disruption. The scene was tense and vividly described, with Rita's prose weaving between the physical act of breaking the dam and the emotional catharsis of reclaiming their power. The first detonation sent a crack through the dam's foundation, and the crowd held its breath. Then another. And another. And then, the roar of water as the first breach was made. The dam, a symbol of everything they had endured, began to crumble.
The flood came, not just of water, but of catharsis, of liberation. The billionaire's empire did not fall that night, but it had been wounded. The young adult stood at the river's edge, watching as the barriers collapsed, as something ancient and free reclaimed its course. The fight was not over. There would be others to take the billionaire's place, new threats cloaked in different guises. But tonight, they had won something real. Not just the river, not just their land, but the undeniable proof that they could fight, and that they could win.

As the floodwaters receded, the young adult walked along the riverbank, their boots sinking into the mud. The air was thick with the scent of wet earth and liberation. And then, emerging from a swirl in the river, an old wooden box and within it, an old cassette tape. It was the kind from the 80s, the kind where people had to be patient to get just the right song off the radio. It sometimes took a long time to get all the songs you wanted, and it was a labor of love. You usually gave it to someone you loved, and it said all the things that needed to be said.

The young adult picked up the tape, turning it over in their hands. It was a relic from a different time, a time when things were slower, when people had to wait for what they wanted. But it was also a reminder of something important: that real change, like a mix tape, takes time and care. It's not something that can be rushed or forced. It's a labor of love, a gift to the future.

The people searched and found an old Walkman radio, its batteries corroded but still functional. They cleaned it up, inserted the tape, and pressed play. The first song began to play, its melody rising over the sound of the river. They didn't know what it was yet, but they could feel it, the perfect anthem for their revolution. It was a song of defiance, of hope, of the unbreakable spirit of those who refuse to bow to tyranny.

And as the music played, the young adult thought about the fight ahead. They thought about the tools they had turned against their oppressors, about the creativity and talent that had fueled their opposition. They thought about the mix tape, about the patience and care it took to create something meaningful. And they knew that their revolution would be the same. It would take time. It would take care. But it would be worth it. Because real change doesn't come from the top down. The top is all part of the greed virus. Real change comes from the bottom up, from the people who have the most to lose and the most to gain. It comes from the artists and the dreamers, the workers and the fighters, the ones who refuse to give up. And it comes from the music, from the songs that remind us who we are and what we're fighting for. The first song played on, its melody rising into the night. And as the young adult listened, they knew that this was just what they were waiting for.

Addendum to Certain Readers

January 31, 2025

Re: New Technology

Dear Progressives & Liberals,

It's time to get over yourselves and this puritanical approach to AI, blockchain, and Bitcoin. Let's be clear: these technologies are not the enemy. They are tools, powerful tools, and like any tool, their value lies in how we choose to wield them. AI is not the end of human creativity; it's the automotive to the horse, the bullet to the arrow. Blockchain is not a fad; it's the computer keyboard to the pen and paper, a new way to record and verify truth. And Bitcoin? It's not just a speculative asset; it's a challenge to the very notion of value, a socialist-style reimagining of how we assign worth in a world dominated by greed. If we don't claim these tools for the people, the billionaire class will use them against us.

Yes, the trappings are often ick. The scamminess, the drooling basement boys, the cringe-worthy meme culture, it's enough to make anyone want to run in the opposite direction. But let's not throw out an entire feast over a single bad dish. Photography didn't replace painting, and the synthesizer didn't replace the piano. These technologies are not here to erase what came before; they're here to expand what's possible.

We need more people, not fewer, willing to use and celebrate these evolutions. Stop being such snobs. Stop clutching your eco conscious pearls and dismissing these tools because of their messianic hype or because their early adopters are insufferable. The future isn't built by those who wait for perfection; it's built by those who roll up their sleeves and get to work.

Imagine what we could do if we embraced these tools instead of fearing them. Open-source cures for cancer, developed collaboratively across borders and institutions. A system of voting and governance that bypasses corrupt politicians, powered by decentralized autonomous organizations (DAOs). Collective governance that protects the planet, its people, and its plants and animals. These aren't pipe dreams; they're possibilities waiting to be realized.

AI can help us solve problems faster and more efficiently than ever before. Blockchain and smart contracts built on it can create systems of transparency and accountability that no single entity can corrupt. Bitcoin and other (though yet to be realized) cryptocurrencies can challenge the monopolies of centralized banks and governments, redistributing power to the people. These technologies are not inherently good or evil, they are what we make of them.

So, let's stop wringing our hands and start using these tools to build the future we want. A future where innovation serves humanity, not just the wealthy. A future where technology is a force for liberation, not oppression. A future where we don't just survive, but thrive.

The time for skepticism is over. The time for action is now. Don't be a snob. Be a builder.

Sincerely,

Humanity, 2025, and the Future

P.S. If you're still on the fence, ask yourself this: Would you rather shape the future, or let it shape you? The choice is yours.

P.P.S. But, but, they use too much energy and are bad for the environment?

Let's talk about that. AI, Bitcoin mining, and blockchain technology do consume energy, but so does every major industry, including traditional banking, data centers, and even Christmas lights (which, by the way, use more electricity annually than some entire countries). The real issue isn't energy consumption itself but the sources of that energy. Already, a significant portion of Bitcoin mining is powered by renewable energy, and advancements in efficiency continue to reduce its environmental impact. Compare this to the carbon footprint of centralized banks, which require massive infrastructure, corporate headquarters, and global financial systems that run on fossil fuels. AI, too, is energy-intensive, but it has the potential to optimize industries in ways that drastically reduce waste and inefficiency. The solution isn't to reject these technologies, it's to ensure they evolve alongside sustainable energy solutions. If we want a greener future, let's fight for better energy policies, not throw out the tools that could help us build that future.

Moreover, Bitcoin's energy use is not a flaw but a feature, its security relies on a decentralized, trustless network that requires computational power to maintain integrity. Unlike traditional financial systems that rely on intermediaries and opaque backroom dealings, Bitcoin ensures trust through its proof-of-work mechanism. The energy it consumes is what keeps it honest, making it resistant to fraud, censorship, and centralized control. This security isn't free, but it's necessary to sustain an independent, decentralized currency. The real question isn't why Bitcoin uses energy, it's why we continue to justify the energy costs of a corrupt financial system that exploits us all.

In Closing
Reciprocity
Our TIDE Revolution

Pat Benatar, *Invincible*, 1985.

As part of the soundtrack to the movie, *The Legend of Billie Jean.*

This bloody road remains a mystery
This sudden darkness fills the air
What are we waiting for?
Won't anybody help us?
What are we waiting for?

We can't afford to be innocent
Stand up and face the enemy
It's a do-or-die situation
We will be invincible

This shattered dream you cannot justify
We're gonna scream until we're satisfied
What are we running for?
We've got the right to be angry
What are we running for?
When there's nowhere we can run to anymore

We can't afford to be innocent
Stand up and face the enemy
It's a do-or-die situation
We will be invincible

And with the power of conviction
There is no sacrifice
It's a do-or-die situation
We will be invincible

Won't anybody help us?

What are we running for
When there's nowhere, nowhere we can run to anymore?

We can't afford to be innocent
Stand up and face the enemy
It's a do-or-die situation
We will be invincible

And with the power of conviction
There is no sacrifice
It's a do-or-die situation
We will be invincible

Yeah (we can't afford to be innocent)
Yeah, yeah (stand up and face the enemy)
(It's a do-or-die situation)
(We will be invincible)

(We can't afford to be innocent)
(Stand up and face the enemy)
(It's a do-or-die situation)
(We will be invincible)

Draw, list, or create any motivating art, music, or culture below:

About EATMS Productions

What's happening to women now is not random. It's structural.

Policy, culture, technology, and power are moving in the same direction.

EATMS maps them clearly and shows how to respond.

This title is part of an ongoing body of work. All EATMS Productions titles, across all series, authors, and formats, are components of a single connected project.

Start here: EATMS System Primer — Free Bundle
https://eatms.gumroad.com/l/dyvzbw

For full catalog or inquiries: eatms.me

Free survival booklet + EATMS updates: email "EATMS" to eatms@pm.me

Please feel free to burn part or all of this book, safely, as an effigy.

www.ingramcontent.com/pod-product-compliance
Lightning Source LLC
Chambersburg PA
CBHW031108250726
48655CB00004B/1623